CW00857512

To wonderful friends who made a big difference:

- Dina Devitantonio, my manager and show's producer, who covered me with generosity and goodness.
- Arlette Beauchamps, my creative publicist.
- Eugenia Macer-Story, a superb author, and source of inspiration.
- Roger Lanoue, Jr., photography and videography genius, who developed my videos and interviews.
- Dr. Sasha Lessin, who enlightened so many.
- Melinda Pomerleau, a gem, a most effective contributor to my work.
- John O'Dowd, one of the best writers in the business.
- Colonel Petrit Demaliaj, who symbolizes the American Dream.

Copyright ©2010 by Maximillien de Lafayette. All rights reserved. No part of this book may be used or reproduced by any means, graphic, electronic, or mechanical, including photocopying, recording, taping or by any information storage retrieval system without the written permission of the author except in the case of brief quotations embodied in critical articles and reviews. Published in November 8, 2010.
Printed in the United States of America. Published by Times Square Press. NY.
Visit the author's website:
www.maximilliendelafayettebibliography.com

Buried History of American Music, Songs and Showbiz Since1606:
The Forgotten Originals, Pioneers, and Mega Stars
Part 2

Based on M. de Lafayette's mega book "The World of Cabaret from 1730 to the Present Day."

Maximillien de Lafayette
Author of The World Who's Who in Jazz, Cabaret, Music and Entertainment
Edited by
Germaine Poitiers
Associate Editor-in-Chief of La Femme Magazine
Veronique Leblanc
Editor-in-Chief of Cabaret Magazine

***   ***   ***

Times Square Press/Elite Associates
New York   California   Paris   London   Tokyo
2010

Table of Contents
Continued from Part 1

Chapter 9: Ragtime and Folk Music...163

Chapter 10: The fabulous soloists of the golden era of the brass bands...185

Chapter 11: An Old New Era...203

Chapter 14: The golden years of live entertainment on radio...267

Chapter 15: Broadway's Vanished Era...303

*** *** ***

Gertie Millar, Countess of Dudley.

Actress and singer. From 1901 to 1910, Gertie Millar was the superstar of the Gaiety Theatre. Nowadays, few remember her famous songs: 'Keep Off the Grass', from The Toreador (1901), 'Berlin Is On The Spree', from The Girls of Gottenberg (1907) and 'Moonstruck' from Our Miss Gibbs (1909).

Gertie Millar was the reigning superstar of the Gaiety Theatre.

Dorothy Dickson. One of the revered figures on the English stage. She lived to be 102.

Dorothy Dickson.

Dorothy Dickson (1893-1995) was billed, without partner, as 'The Greatest Dance Personality in the World.'
This extravagant claim attracted Ziegfeld who hired her as featured dancer in the 1917 Follies. She teamed with Hyson again for Jerome Kern's 'Rock-a-bye Baby,' yet her success was so pronounced that the New York Times on May 26, 1918, ran a feature announcing her as the successor of Irene Castle as the mistress of ballroom dancing.

*** *** ***

Margaret Livingston

Florence Hedges

Lenore Ulric

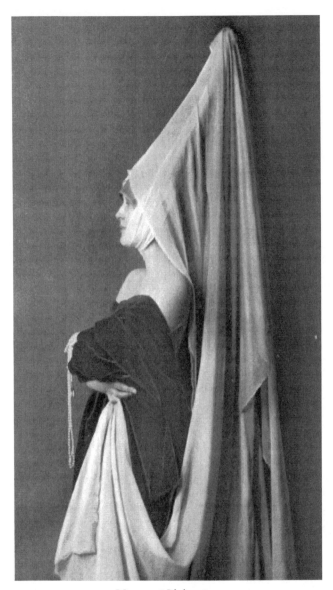

Margaret Livingston

Imogene Wilson

Violet Heming

Geraldine Farrar

Lili (Lily) Damita. She was a big big name!!

27

Lili (Lily) Damita

Gina Malo

Ada May

Ruby Keeler, wife of Al Jolson.

Born in 1910 in Nova Scotia, Ruby Keeler moved to New York with her family in 1912. Soon enrolled in the Professional Children's School, she eventually found her way to Broadway and the pivotal role in *42nd Street*. She was soon one of the most popular actresses in Hollywood. Her performance in "No, No, Nanette", in 1971, her first Broadway show in 41 years, met with rave reviews. (Data: Nancy Marlow)

Alice Terry and Alex Ingram.

Alice Terry

Ann Penington

Ann Pennington (1893-1971) was the greatest of the solo female
stage dancers on Broadway (1910s and '20s)!

Catherine Dale Owen
Catherine Dale Owen (1903-1965) A Kentuckian educated at the
American Academy of Dramatic Arts, Catherine Dale Owen
combined superlative beauty with a graceful stage manner. As an

eighteen-year old student, Owen became the special project of Mrs. Frank Gilmore, the executive secretary of Actors Equity, who engineered her Broadway launch in 1921's "Happy Go Lucky." An ingénue, Owen quickly made a mark, appearing in "The Bootleggers" (1922) and "The Whole Town's Talking" (1923).

In 1925, she was named one of the ten most beautiful women in the world.

Her stage career climaxed in the Ferenc Molnar hit, "The Play's the Thing" (1926-1927). From 1924 until 1928 she made repeated screen tests without being signed as a lead. The coming of sound made her refined speaking style an advantage. John Gilbert lobbied to obtain her as lead for "His Glorious Night."

Gilbert's first sound feature became one of the infamous films of the era of the transition to sound, a stilted costume drama that killed his career.

Though Owen's acting in the film is curiously lifeless, she was sufficiently photogenic to survive for two years in Hollywood, appearing in seven further features, mediocre items with high culture overtones.

The best of these is the now lost operetta, "The Rogue Song," that marked the film premiere of singer Lawrence Tibbett. She married stock broker Milton F. Davis, Jr. in 1934, divorced him in 1937, and remarried advertising executive Homer Metzger. (His/Data: Broadway.cas.sc.edu)

*** *** ***

Catherine Dale Owen

Louise Brooks:
An unforgettable character of the era
(Nov. 14,1906-Aug. 8, 1985)

Lots of ink and verses were poured into Hollywood chronicles of scandals, trashing people, jeopardizing careers, ruining marriages and families...and ironically, launching the careers of some. Sometimes, a scandal puts an end to star's career, but quite often, it catapults the rise of aspiring artists, starlets and stars. Scandal is a sword with a double-edge; either it cuts your throat, or breaks through impregnable barriers. Some have used the casting couch, others, the influence of wealthy and powerful old *grand seigneurs* who were fond of young girls and soft silky skin.

In all cases, the actress and the diva in the making had to return the favors by engaging in sexual acts, and sharing partners, on the set, off the set, in the dressing room, even in wives' boudoirs. Sex, was their meal ticket. Talent was not a prerequisite to start a career, rather, a dignified way to end it. Sinatra said:"Luck is 99% of the whole deal, talent comes much much later." In our scenario, sex is 99% of the whole deal, and luck is 1%.

Many disagree.

But life is not always built upon objectivity, in Hollywood, subjectivity is a *force majeure*. Who fits this bill? Many. And by many, I mean thousands of female stars who managed to shine, permanently or briefly.

And the living examples abound, starting with Alla Nazimova, Theda Bara, Marion Davies, Jean Harlow, Joan Crawford, Clara Bow, and Louise Brooks. But Louise Brooks is on the top of my list...for now.

Sex was a game and a necessity to Brooks, and conjugal fidelity meant nothing to her.

Louise Brooks is unique.

An enigmatic character blended with sophistication, elegance, panache, intelligence, finesse, an exemplary loyalty to friends (But not to lovers or husbands!!), generosity, sarcasm, defiance, and insatiable sex appetite. And this appetite was disturbing quite a bit, because she could not function without having sexual partners around the clock.

A notorious, yet well respected French columnist, once said to me: "Louise c'est comme un ciseaux...il faut l'ouvrir pour que ca fonctionne." Translation: "Louise is like a pair of scissor. You got to open it to make it work." He meant that Louise had to spread her legs wide open to achieve what she has achieved on the screen and on stage. And Louise did! And quite often.

With his Parisian sarcasm, Jean Nohain once told me verbatim: "Every lover she had wanted to spend the rest of his life between her legs, but not a single minute as a wife." He meant, no one would trust her as a wife, because she was addicted to sex with multiple partners! Despite her scandalous affairs, Louise Brooks took Paris by storm, and the French adored her! C'est la vie!

Sex at fourteen!

"It is doubtful any film actress in the nineteen-twenties displayed a greater sense of overt sexuality on screen and off screen than Louise Brooks," said a commentator.

Louise's insatiable sex appetite, infidelity, and erotic curiosity got her into hot waters.

At fourteen, and as a nude model, she lost her virginity to a painter, who enjoyed her defloration with a number of other boys who were present at his studio. Louise Brooks did them all.
Willingly or unwillingly, sex maniac Louise Brooks inaugurated her sex life with a group sex!
She admitted that event in her diary. One year later, Louise was offered a small job in a touring dance troupe.
Two days later, Brooks began to sleep with the publicist of the troupe. Because of her obsession with sex, and constant demands for more sex, the publicist nicknamed her the "Hell Cat."

He begged for mercy, for Brooks has consumed all his physical energy, but Brooks kept on asking for more sex. Soon, gossip and rumors began to circulate about her nymphomania, and the multiple gang-bang sessions she had with the entire backstage crew. Brooks was fired.
Following the advice of a friend, Brooks moved to New York, looking for a job as dancer. She landed on the net of George White, who was notorious for producing risqué and nudity shows on Broadway.
Worth mentioning here that White was arrested twice on charge of obscenity, and the district attorney shut down (Twice) his show, and his vice squad arrested some of his female stars during the premiere.
The same thing happened also to Earl Carroll, and to his "Vanities" show in 1924, and two of his female stars were booked for obscenity.
Welcome to the club, Dear Louise.

*** *** ***

Louise Brooks in New York: A call-girl with unorthodox habits and lots of sex.

In New York, Louise Brooks met the who's who of New York silky society. And her favorite men were the rich and powerful old ones. Ironically, Louise Brooks admitted that young men were far more exciting, but the older gentlemen procured her peace and stability. She meant by stability, financial security, jewels, furs, diamonds and a ritzy apartment. And Louise got them all.

In her mind, being sexually active, and sharing multiple lovers, and sexual partners was not an immoral conduct, on the contrary, to Louise, sex was an effective way of communicating with others, inspirational, and even necessary for her creativity. And working as an escort or a call girl did not offend her morality, as long as, she had the last word.

In New York, during the twenties and the thirties, it was customary in showbiz to throw elaborate parties for the "elder gentlemen" who poured their money in a show production. And parties meant, lots of skin, and lots of gorgeous stars and starlets solely invited to entertain the "dignitaries", and the aging angels. Simply put, Louise Brooks was both an artist and a sophisticated whore.

In her biography, Louise Brooks wrote: "In New York, there was a hand-picked group of beautiful girls who were invited to parties given for great men in finance and government. We had to be fairly well bred and of absolute integrity, never endangering the great men with threats of publicity or blackmail. At these parties we were not required, like common whores, to go to bed with any man who asked us, but if we did the profits were great. Money, jewels, mink coats, a film job, you name it."

In New York City, Louise Brooks stayed at the Algonquin Hotel. And Lord Beaverbrook picked up the tab.

He was crazy about her. He covered her with jewels and gifts. Despite his generosity, Brooks never really cared about him. In fact, she described him as an ugly monkey who had no manners. While the Lord was paying all her extravagant bills, Brooks was seeing a fleet of men. A chambermaid described her room as a bordello. The hotel management had no other choice than to kick her out. She moved to another hotel in Manhattan, and once again, she was asked to leave.

45

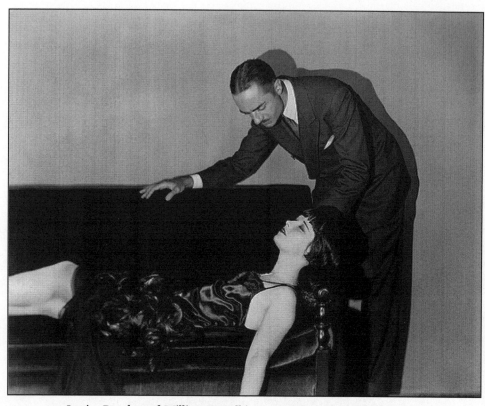

Louise Brooks and William Powell in a scene from the 1929 film "The
Canary Murder Case." Right, also from the same picture.
She was magnificent!

From one man to another...constantly!

Photo: Flo Ziegfeld.

Because of her scandalous reputation, Brooks had to leave New York. People nicknamed her the "Nymphomaniac Vampire." Brooks settled for a while in Paris, where she took her audience and showbiz milieu by storm. The French adored her.

She appealed to their taste; she was elegant, spoke French, and knew the French etiquette.

In fact, she was well-read, and knew a lot about the French poets, Parisian literature, haute couture, and the pre-existentialist movement.

Many thought she was French.

In Paris, Louise Brooks had multiple threesomes with the legendary French-Armenian photographer Demirjian, and high class prostitutes of his choice. A few months later, she received a telegram from Flo Ziegfeld, offering her a leading role in his extravagant "Follies." She packed up and returned to New York. Brooks was well paid, but not well enough to carry on and maintain the standard of her debaucherie.

Prostitution and posing naked were added to her curriculum to cover her expenses and to support her outrageous life style. She had a brief affair with Ziegfeld, but this "old rabbit" as she called him could not satisfy her. During one of her escapades, she met a multi-millionaire character by the name of John Lock. She moved into his ritzy apartment, and like Lord Beaverbrook, he showered her with diamonds and gifts. But it was hard for Brooks to kick out her old nasty habit. She needed more men on a daily basis. Lock caught her in the act with screenwriter Martin Townsend. Lock went ape, when Louise asked him to undress and join in. Lock kicked her out.

Photos from L to R, Brooks' lovers: 1. Walter Wanger.
2. Lord Beaverbrook.

Brooks did not mind for a while, because a third man (Married with three children and a highly respected wife) was waiting for her. Brooks moved in a third apartment fully paid by Martin. Mon Dieu, men never learn! Martin was well connected.
He introduced her to Walter Wanger, who was in charge of shows production at the Players Lasky. Martin regretted it later, when he learned that Brooks was sleeping with Walter Wanger. How did she get the job? Easy.
According to Nigel Cawthorne, "At the interview in his office, Wanger asked Louise what made her think she had what it took to make it in the movies. She took off her clothes, lay down on the couch and showed him."
Boom kaboom, Brooks got a contract, and moved with Wanger to Hollywood. So far, and in less than three months, Brooks had already slept with five men, in addition to several secret lovers.

Louise Brooks in Hollywood: More sexual partners and lesbianism orgies.

In Hollywood, Louise Brook's sexual appetite exploded. Her first two sexual partners were William Powell and Charlie Chaplin.
One of her most notorious affairs was her threesome with the "Little Rat" Charlie Chaplin (As she called him) and lesbian Peggy Fears.

During one of her multiple orgies with Peggy Fears, Louise Brooks met A. Blumenthal, a well-known figure of the motion pictures industry. Brooks left Chaplin for Blumenthal, but occasionally, she would see Chaplin en cachette. But once she discovered that Chaplin had a venereal disease, Brooks dumped him for good.

Notorious lesbian, Peggy Fears, Louise Brooks' sexual partner in steamy orgies with Charlie Chaplin.

Photo: Louise Brooks with director/future husband Eddie Sutherland.
She divorced in June 1928.

According to Cawthorne, "At the time, Chaplin was convinced that iodine prevented VD. One night at the Ambassador Hotel, he painted his entire genitalia and came charging at Louise and Peggy Fears with a bright red erection."

Brooks had enough of Charlie Chaplin and William Powell. She began a new affair with director Eddie Sutherland, who was married at the time. They stayed together for two months, and got married. Soon after, she fell madly in love with actor Buster Collier, who according to her diary, was the love of her life. While still dating Collier, behind the back of her husband, Brooks started a discreet affair with actress Constance Talmadge.

The woman is insatiable! Her infidelity and sex-mania did not stop here. Now Louise Brooks began to experience a foursome. New sexual partners were added to her soupe du jour. One of them was George Preston Marshall, owner of a chain of laundries and future owner of the Washington Redskins football team. About him, Brooks said: "The most fateful encounter of my life." Then, something strange and very unusual happened. Brooks promised Marshall that she will be loyal to him, and she will never again fool around. A promise, Brooks never gave to any of the 150 men she slept with. Well, that's promising.

But will Brooks keep her promise? Far from it. A few days later, Brooks was found in bed with Greta Garbo.

Marlene Dietrich heard about it and rushed to invite Brooks – allegedly to talk about Dimirjian—and the two ended digging into each other. "It was awesome," later on, Brooks will comment on her affair with Dietrich. Rumors about her affairs with Garbo and Dietrich began to circulate in Hollywood. The very graphic rumors caught the attention of another notorious lesbian, Pepi Lederer (Marion Davies' niece.) Well well!

What did happen to Brooks' promise to Marshall? Gone with the wind, folks. Lederer became Brooks' newest sexual partner.

Lederer was delighted, and she began to brag about her affair with Brooks. Jack Pickford was all ears.

He heard all the juicy details from Lederer. This was a big mistake on the part of Lederer, because a few days later, she caught Brooks giving oral sex to Pickford! Worth mentioning here, that Louise Brooks was still married to Eddie Sutherland.

But this one was not an angel, either, for he was sleeping with several actresses, and an avalanche of Hollywood's beauties, including Bebe Daniels.

The couple divorced, and Brooks returned to George Preston Marshall. In 1933, she married Chicago millionaire Deering Davis, but abruptly left him in March 1934 after only five months of marriage, "without a good-bye... and leaving only a note of her intentions" behind her. According to Card, Davis was just "another elegant, well-heeled admirer," nothing more.

The couple officially divorced in 1938, as reported by Squidoo.

One day, Clara Bow who also had an affair with Brooks, called her to let her know that George Marshall was fooling around. She advised her to get rid of him. Bow suggested to Brooks, that she should focus her attention on Ben Schulberg, the big boss of Paramount.

Brooks went to see Schulberg, a shrewd, tough cookie. And as expected, Brooks spread her legs wide open, hoping that her sexual talent would do the trick. It did not. Schulberg enjoyed the view, serviced the hungry slut, and promised to call her the very next morning. He never did.

*** *** ***

Photo: George Preston Marshall, in front of the Red Skins office.

Notorious lesbian, Pepi Lederer. (Marion Davies' niece.)

Facts about this most unusual woman:

- After an unsuccessful attempt at operating a dance studio, she returned East and, after brief stints as a radio actor and a gossip columnist, worked as a salesgirl in a Saks Fifth Avenue store in New York City for a few years, then eked out a living as a courtesan with a few select wealthy men as clients.
- Brooks unfortunately had a life-long love of alcohol (more specifically gin), having begun drinking heavily at the age of fourteen and was an alcoholic for a major portion of her life.
- She was a notorious spendthrift for most of her life, even filing for bankruptcy once, but was kind and generous to her friends, almost to a fault.
- Despite her two marriages, she never had children, referring to herself as "Barren Brooks."
- Her many lovers from years before had included a young William S. Paley, the founder of CBS. According to Louise Brooks, Paley provided a small monthly stipend to Brooks for the rest of her life, and according to the documentary this stipend kept her from committing suicide at one point.
- George Marshall was the biggest reason she was able to secure a contract with Pabst. Marshall repeatedly asked her to marry him and after finding that she had had many affairs while they were together, married film actress Corinne Griffith instead.
- French film historians rediscovered her films in the early 1950s, proclaiming her as an actress who surpassed even Marlene Dietrich and Greta Garbo as a film icon (Henri Langlois: "There is no Garbo, there is no Dietrich, there is only Louise Brooks!"), much to her amusement.
- James Card, the film curator for the George Eastman House, discovered Louise living as a recluse in New York City, and persuaded her to move to Rochester, New York to be near the George Eastman House film collection. With his help, she became a noted film writer in her own right. A collection of her witty and cogent writings, "Lulu in Hollywood," was published in 1982.

- She rarely gave interviews, but had special relationships with John Kobal and Kevin Brownlow, the film historians, and they were able to capture on paper some of her amazing personality.
- She had lived alone by choice for many years, and Louise Brooks died from a heart attack in 1985, after suffering from arthritis and emphysema for many years.
- Brooks is considered one of the first naturalistic actors in film's history.
- She made her movie debut in 1925 for Paramount Pictures, and appeared in eleven films in less than three years starring opposite major stars such as W.C. Fields, and Adolphe Menjou.
- Brooks had always been very self-directed, even difficult, and was notorious for her salty language, which she didn't hesitate to use whenever she felt like it. In addition, she had made a vow to herself never to smile on stage unless she felt compelled to, and although the majority of her publicity photos show her with a neutral expression, she had a dazzling smile. By her own admission, she was a sexually liberated woman, not afraid to experiment, even posing fully nude for "art" photography, and her liaisons with many film people were legendary, although much of it is speculation.
- She described Garbo as masculine but a "charming and tender lover."
- She said: "When I am dead, I believe that film writers will fasten on the story that I am a lesbian. I have done lots to make it believable...All my women friends have been lesbians. But that is one point upon which I agree positively with Christopher Isherwood: There is no such thing as bisexuality. Ordinary people, although they may accommodate themselves for reason of whoring or marriage, are one-sexed. Out of curiosity, I had two affairs with girls - they did nothing for me."
- She was considered the most elegant star of the silent films era, and Hollywood golden age.
- She was one of the most photographed celebrities of her time.
- She was arrested in Kansas for lewd cohabitation. A term for adultery.

- She was kicked out of Kansas, flat broke.
- Went back to New York City and became the mistress of millionaire Sam Colt.
- Sam Colt got rid of her, because she continued to sleep with other men.
- Bisexual Tallulah Bankhead took her in. She sheltered her. And of course, the two became lovers.
- Bankhead got tired of her and asked her to leave her apartment. Brooks became a prostitute.
- She made no public apologies for preferring sex, and alcohol to a steady job.
- She said, "I have a gift for enraging people, but if I ever bore you, it'll be with a knife."
- She said, "I learned how to act by watching Martha Graham dance, and I learned how to dance by watching Charlie Chaplin act."
- About Berlin, Brooks wrote: "Sex was the business of the town. At the Eden Hotel, where I lived, the café bar was lined with the higher-priced trollops. The economy girls walked the street outside. On the corner stood the girls in boots, advertising flagellation. Actors' agents pimped for the ladies in luxury apartments in the Bavarian quarter. Racetrack touts at the Hoppegarten arranged orgies for groups of sportsmen. The nightclub Eldorado displayed an enticing line of homosexuals dressed as women. At the Maly, there was a choice of feminine or collar-and-tie lesbians."
- With a spate of popular Hollywood films under her belt including *The Show-Off* (1926), *A Girl In Every Port* (1928) and *Beggars Of Life* (1928), she thumbed her nose at Paramount and broke her contract to star in what would be her two greatest films, *Pandora's Box (Die Buchse der Pandora)* and *Diary of a Lost Girl (Das Tagebuch Einer Verlorenen)*, both with German director G. W. Pabst in 1929. These two films would elevate a good director to near-legendary status, make a cultural icon out of Brooks and virtually destroy the rest of her acting career in the process. Returning to Hollywood in 1931, she was relegated to supporting roles and B movies, before retiring in obscurity less than ten years later, as stated by David Jeffers.

- On August 8, 1985, Louise Brooks was found dead of a massive heart attack. She was buried in Holy Sepulchre Cemetery in Rochester, New York, as reported by Squidoo.

*** *** ***

Louise Brooks' lovers and sexual partners:

It was said that Brooks has slep with more than 150 men, and explored all sorts and types of sex, ranging from one night stand to group sex, and from straight sex to lesbianism. Among her most notorious sexual partners were (Just to name a few):

- A.C. Blumental.
- Alla Nazimova.
- Bebe Daniels.
- Ben Schulberg.
- Buster Collier.
- Charlie Chaplin.
- Clara Bow.
- Claudette Colbert.
- Constance Talmadge.
- Danny Aikman, a notorious nude model and bisexual.
- Deering Davis, a Chicago millionaire.
- Dimirhian, a French-Armenian photographer.
- Dorothy MacKaill.
- Dorothy Knapp.
- Earl Carroll.
- Eddie Sutherland (She married him).
- Fletcher Crandall, a crook.
- Flo Ziegfeld.
- George Preston Marshall.
- George W. Pabst, the German film-maker who took her under his wing in Germany, and launched her career in Europe. She was his mistress for 3 weeks. Then left him for Sepp Allgeier, his cameraman.
- George White.
- Gloria Swanson.
- Greta Garbo.

- Gustav Diessel, the German actor who co-starred with her in the Pandora Box. Louise played Lulu. In that film, Brooks and Diessel engaged into real sex. The film was banned in France and Germany for reason of obscenity. It contained real scenes of kinky sex, incest, and lesbianism.
- Humphrey Bogart.
- Jack Pickford.
- Jack Randall, a singing cowboy.
- James Card, a married man who was a photography curator at Kodak.
- James Dunne, a married Irish businessman in New York.
- Joan Crawford.
- John Kobal, a film historian.
- John Lock.
- John Wayne.
- Josephine Baker.
- Kevin Brownlow, a film historian.
- Lord Beaverbrook.
- Marlene Dietrich.
- Martin Townsend.
- Peggy Fears.
- Pepi Lederer.
- Rene Clair, French film-maker.
- Sam Colt, co-owner of the Colt guns company.
- Sepp Allgeier, a German cameraman.
- Tallulah Bankhead.
- Valeska Get, who introduced her to lesbians' orgies circles in Berlin.
- Walter Wanger.
- William Powell.
- William S. Paley, the founder of CBS.

George W. Pabst, the German film-maker who took her under his wing
in Germany, and launched her career in Europe.

Louise Brooks with John Wayne.

Olga Petrova

Evangeline Raleigh (1906-19??) Voted "Miss Broadway of 1927".

Anita Page

With sincere
appreciation
Anita Page

Anita Page

Pauline Frederick

Ona Munson

Her suicide note said, 'This is the only way I know to be free again.'

Geraldine Ferrar

Geraldine Ferrar (1882-1967)--American opera diva and silent film star, Geraldine Ferrar, was one of the most famous women in the world during the second decade of the 20th century. Beautiful, stylish, and possessed of enormous charisma, her presence mattered as much as her voice in her stardom. While the surviving sound recordings reveal an expressive and elegant lyric soprano voice that can sing in four languages idiomatically (a testament to her solid training by Emanuel Garcia), none of the performances have the drama or beauty of tone that compel fascination 90 years later. (Data:: Broadway.cas.sc.edu)

Gilda Ray

Renée Adorée. She was adored by millions!!

Armida

Agnes Ayres

Vilma Banky

Sally Blane

Eleanor Boardman

Olive Borden

Virginia Bradford

Betty Bronson

June Clyde

June Collyer

Betty Compson

María Cordá

Viola Dana

Margueritte De La Motte

Marian Douglas (Ena Gregory)

Carol McComas

Josephine Dunn

Daisy Irving

Sedley, a top model of the era, 1903.

Dorothy Dwan

Lina Cavalieri. One of the most elegant women of her time.

Sally Eilers

93

Ruth Elder

Audrey Ferris

Helen Foster

Betty Furness

Leila Hyams

Beth Laemmle

Jacqueline Logan

Shirley Mason

Marilyn Morgan (Marian Marsh)

Gertrude Olmstead

Marie Prevost

Esther Ralston. Considered one of the most beautiful women of the era.

Ann Rork

Constance Talmadge (1897-1973). Yes sir! She was very very famous!!

Thelma Todd (1905-1935). She made big headlines!

Claire Windsor

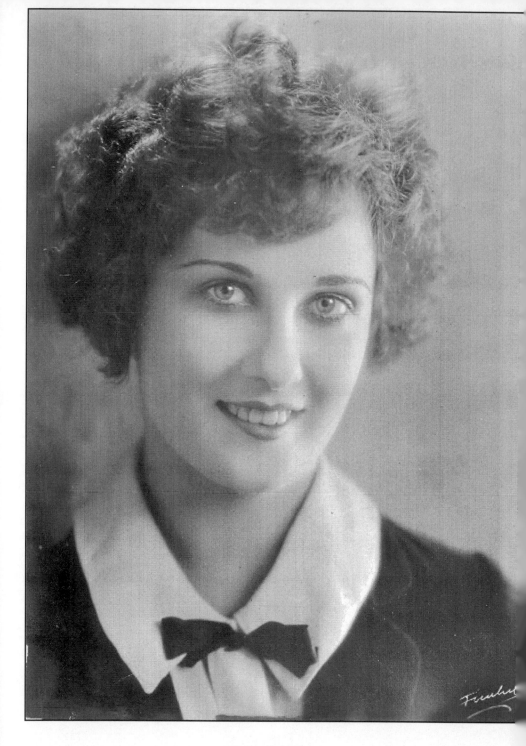

Barbara Worth

Fay Wray (1904-2007). One of the greatest legends of showbiz!

Gilda Ray

Phyllis Dare (1887-1975)
She was one of the most popular picture-postcard beauties of the
Edwardian era.

Alice Delysia

Olive May (née Olive Mary Meatyard), Countess of Drogheda.

Billie Carleton

Billie Carleton, born Florence Lenora Stewart, was part of a fast-living, drug-taking set. After an all-night party following a Victory Ball at the Albert Hall in November 1918, she was found dead in bed, the victim of a drugs overdose. Her cocaine supplier was sent to jail. The Tatler had reviewed one of her appearances: 'She has cleverness, temperament and charm. Not enough of the first, and perhaps too much of the latter.' Her death inspired several plays and films most notably Nöel Coward's The Vortex, 1924. As reported by NPG.

Gaby Deslys. A French Legend!

Famously extravagant dancer and singer. Gaby Deslys made her debut in 1906, at the Gaiety Theatre in 1906. Gordon Selfridge gave her a gift that made headlines in the papers: A rope of rare pearls as long as her height. Her last memorable stage appearance was in 1918, at the Casino de Paris, in Laissez-les Tomber!

Gaby Deslys

Gaby Deslys

Gaby Deslys

Anna May Wong. A superb actress, victimized by studios' bosses,
because she was Chinese!

Camille Clifford

Dorothy Minto

Gabrielle Ray (née Gabrielle Elizabeth Clifford Cook) as Polly Polino in
'Peggy'.

Gabrielle Ray

King Edward VII and Queen Alexandra were in the Royal Box, and witnessed Miss Ray's apparition as Thisbe. W. Macqueen-Pope wrote, 'The house gave a gasp of admiration...a new Gaiety star was born...and when she appeared in pink pyjamas and danced in them, every young man's head was awhirl'. Interviewed a few months later, 'Gabs' Ray said, 'I am always dancing; I love it! When I don't dance, I sing. What else is there to do?' (Data: Thisbe. W. Macqueen-Pop, NPG)

Fritzi Scheff demonstrating Magnavox for Fifth Liberty Loan in New
York City, 1895.

Fritzi Scheff was a very big name in the business!

She loved cars. Fritzi in 1913.

Jessie Reed

Jessie Reed

Lilyan Tashman. She was a MEGA star!!

The Legendary Marie Dressler!!

David S. Shields said: "Marie Dressler (1868-1934) No one embodied
feminine rage with quite the volcanic physicality of Marie Dressler."

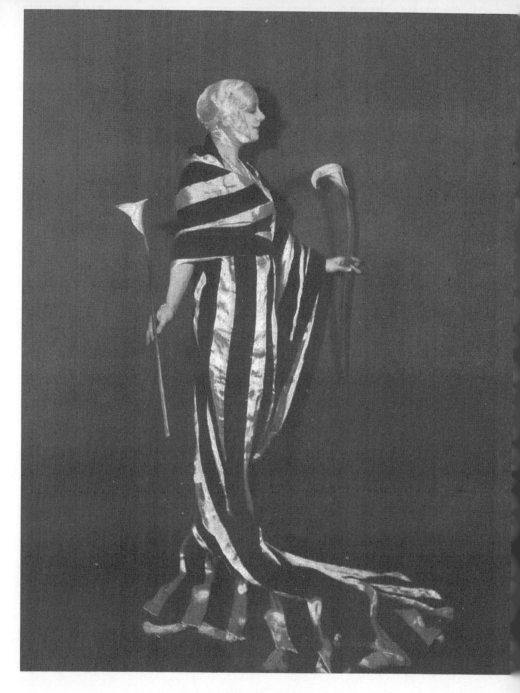

Irene Bordoni

Brigitte Helm

Jane Green

"Singin The Blues" Vitaphone short. Martha Jane Greene with second husband Ron Wilson at the piano in 1928.

Ruth Chatterton (1893 1961)

Remembered for her roles in "Madame X" and "Dodsworth".

Marion Harris in 1917. One of America's most successful and famous singers of the Golden Era!

Marion Harris in 1933.

Corinne Griffith

Adrianne Allen

Rose Dolores (1892-1975). She was the most famous Ziegfeld Girl.

Mary Miles Minter. She made headlines!!

Katherine Alexander

Mary Eaton (1901-1948) was Florenz Ziegfeld's successor to Marilyn
Miller as the premier dancer in the Follies.

Enid Bennett

She shined and vanished!

Nita Naldi

Adele Astaire (Fred Astaire's Sister, who taught him how to dance.)

Phyllis Haver

Theda Bara. One of the earliest and greatest stars of Hollywood!!

Pola Negri. At one time in Hollywood's history, Negri was larger than any screen. One of the closest friends of Rudolph Valentino.

Scene from Earl Carroll's "Vanities", then...the most scandalous show in the country, starring Peggy Hopkins Joyce, then, the most notorious woman in America. Sophie Tucker, the "last of the red-hot Mommas," sang in the show. The show did not have household names, and no celebrated singers and performers. Without name recognition, Carroll had to feature nudity on a grand scale to sell tickets. Voila!

1924 Most Notorious Woman in America
Fantasy in the 1920s...vice squad...gorgeous
girls...fabulous legs and delighted audience...

Earl Carroll's 1924 "Vanities" starring Peggy Hopkins Joyce, then the most notorious woman in America opened on September 10th and ran for 440 performances. It was the most scandalous show in the country, because nudity was a common element in "Vanities." The show catered to the so-called "busy and tired businessmen" by displaying "gorgeous legs", bared breasts, and parading 108 beautiful showgirls as peacocks at the sensual tempo of Ravel's "Bolero."

151

Earl Carroll explained: "The aesthetic art of the number demands that the girls be in the absolute buff this time, not even G-strings." Leon Whipple in The Survey Magazine, March issue, 1926, described the show, its artists and performers, and the public reaction as follows: "For a not excessive price, men, women, and adolescents can go into a lovely New York theatre on Broadway and see naked bodies, generally of women, under full lights with nothing on save what antique writers call a "zone"(belt or girdle). The rest of the body is completely and absolutely nude, with scarce alleviation of a coat powder. The bodies are exposed as statues, figurines, and symbolic persons, with recurrent veilings and for brief flashes.

The showmanship is deft and even discreet though the shadowy lighting of yesteryear has given way to the full flood. The exposure of the body lasts probably five minutes out of the three hours, though there is a constant and cloying stream of lesser bareness — legs, backs, torsos, and anatomical odds and ends. To these latter we have already been acclimated for the unveiling has been going on in New York for several years, almost by fractions of inches as the producers tried out the public taste. Indeed, the student might find a thesis in social science in the scrutiny of this process of breaking down a convention by annual innovation. — Not Art and Not Model." (Source: Will A. Page, Behind the Curtains of the Broadway Beauty Trust, 1927)

Earl Carroll's "Vanities" show: Problem with the D.A., and New York Vice Squad!

New York City District Attorney did not like Carroll's decision. The New York Vice Squad was alerted. The next morning the D.A. demanded that Carroll should clothe the performers. Carroll refused. On September 11th, a police officer stood in the wings of the theatre ready to stop any nudity act, and brought with him several blankets. The show opened with Kathryn Ray "in the buff" swinging upside down over an enormous clock. The officer rushed to the stage attempting to capture Ray and cover her with his blanket. But as agile as a rabbit, Ray broke free and vanished behind the stage.

The risqué and very controversial poster of Kathryn Ray

Peggy Hopkins Joyce. Born Marguerite Upton in 1893 to Berkley barber Sam Upton and his wife Dora Wood. Peggy Joyce ran away from home in 1910 and rapidly she gained fame, and fortune, as Carroll's "stage nude performer", and later as Ziegfeld's showgirl. Later on, she became famous for her many marriages to millionaires. She died in 1957.

The audience thought it was part of the show! They loved this scene and applauded like maniacs. Meanwhile, the police officer was still chasing Kathryn Ray.

Two stagehands finally rescued Ray by getting her out of the theater from the stage back door. The curtain fell, and the audience was still applauding! Short after, Earl Carroll stepped forward to tell the delighted audience, that the D.A. and the Board of Censors are trying to shut down his show.

The audience became furious and many of the "busy and tired businessmen" who were watching the show were indeed powerful and had connections in high places.

They assured Carroll that the show will go on. In fact, The Board of Censors lost its battle in a landslide *cause celebre,* and the show went on. Kathryn Ray became a celebrity overnight. The very next morning, waves of teenaged boys rushed to the lobby of the theatre to buy the poster of naked Kathryn Ray that was displayed in a prominent place in the lobby of the theater and strategically positioned to attract more people. And out of nowhere, the officer who tried once to catch Ray resurfaced again in the lobby, screaming and yelling at Carroll.

The police officer ordered him to remove Ray's huge poster. And as usual, Carroll refused. The furious policeman arrested Carroll on a charge of public obscenity. Carroll found himself on trial on November 10, 1924 for displaying obscene posters.

The three judge panel of the Court of Special Sessions retired to consider their verdict which, they announced, would be based strictly upon the question of fact: Were the images immoral? "We have examined the exhibits that are specimens of nudity and find they are not sufficient to hold the defendant. We find the defendant should be acquitted." W.C. Fields, who starred in several of Carroll's later revues, reached his own verdict: "Earl Carroll is a preacher with an erection." Lincoln Steffens might have found him an "honest crook."

The premiere muckraking journalist of the Progressive Era, Steffens claimed to prefer "honest crooks," rascals who admitted their rascality so long as the admission could not be used against them in a court of law, over do-gooders of any sort.

At least with an "honest crook" you got the truth. Carroll began his statement to the judges by saying "I have always staked my name, my reputation, and when I had it, my money, on the conception of what people wanted to see."

He never pretended that the "Vanities" had any higher purpose than giving the audience what it craved. This was, in a word, titilation." He won, and the show went on for another 438 performances. Meanwhile, and in many states in America, vice squads were cracking down on beauties bathing in revealing swimsuits...Women's beach suits were "censored!"

In that time in history, the great majority of young American women did not participate in a bathing beauty contest.

But thousands of them did go to beaches where their outfits and swimsuits raised the moral issues, Carroll faced.

Faith Bacon:

Faith Bacon was the most beautiful woman in the world (according to Florenz Ziegfeld) and the supposed inventor of the fan dance. When she was 20, Faith Bacon got a job in Broadway, as a chorus girl in Earl Carroll's *Vanities of 1930*. Carroll, a big time Broadway producer who, in his day, gloried in the snappy nickname, "the picker of pulchritude", was anxious to come up with a new way of getting some naked female flesh up on stage as part of the show.

Faith Bacon

In New York, it was legal to have nude women on stage as long as they didn't move, so shows often featured artistic tableaux with an array of stationary nudes.

However, that wasn't good enough for the pulchritude picker, who found himself in a creative crisis.

There had to be a novel way of flashing some skin without getting arrested! At this moment of emergency, according to Faith's publicist -- clearly a fan of *42nd Street* (1933) -- "a chorine stepped out of line and offered a suggestion."

It was Faith, of course, taking a reckless chance to pitch her idea to the top man. "Mr. Carroll," she said, "Why can't we do a number where I'm covered when I move, and undraped when I stop? For example -- let's say the orchestra plays a waltz. I dance around, but on every third note, the music stops and I stand still and uncover!"

Carroll was impressed, and asked what she thought she could use to cover herself during the waltzing interludes. She suggested that ostrich feathers would be ideal, and so the fan dance – truly, the zenith of American pre-war culture – was born.

Faith toured America for the next few years, standing still on every third note, getting lots of ink in the gossip pages and occasionally getting busted by the police for outraging public decency, as mentioned in More than you need to know; King Feature Syndicate, 1938, and The Hammond Times, February 25 1937.

*** *** ***

A beach censor arresting two women in Chicago in 1922 for violating the laws concerning proper beach attire.

Sex, old men and gold diggers.

Just as Solomon could scarcely have "been very intimate" with most of his wives, the well-to-do New Yorker, or the anyone "above penury" who watched those naked women on stage, could not romance all one hundred or so beauties on stage at the Follies or the Vanities or Scandals.

An unlucky few "tired businessmen" fell for a particular girl.
The most notable, because most unfortunate, was Stanley Joyce, Peggy Hopkins' third husband whose one-year marriage with the decade's most celebrated "gold digger" cost him at least two million dollars. Indeed she entitled one chapter of her autobiography, *Men, Marriage, and Me* (1930) which described one week in her marriage to Joyce, "How to Spend a Million a Week."
Will Page devoted several chapters of *Behind The Curtains* to stories of rich men taken for large sums by the "gold diggers" of the chorus.

Earl Carroll with his girls.

Gilda Gray

One admirer of Gilda Gray, for example, tossed a diamond
bracelet worth $100,000 onto the stage to show his appreciation.

Dorothy Knapp, another star of the Earl Carroll's show "Vanities" whom Carroll had billed as "the most beautiful girl in the world" and whose costume supplies a useful definition of what Page meant by the "minimum" worn by "the rest of the comely cast."

Chapter 9
Ragtime and Folk Music

- Historical background
- Ernest Hogan
- Sheet music of "The Cake-Walk In The Sky"
- Lyrics of the song: All Coons look alike to me
- Ragtime: An important part of American culture
- Some of the most important songs were
- The most popular songs of the era were
- Tom Turpin
- Cakewalks in the ragtime era
- First published composition with the word "cakewalk"
- All time favorites
- The 50 most popular tunes
- List of the most popular songs
- Ragtime women composers
- The work of early female songwriters
- Famous female composers

*** *** ***

Chapter 9
Ragtime and Folk Music

The Cakewalk, a predecessor of the rag, is best known from 1870 to the early 20th century, but it took its roots from the time of slavery. White slave owners used to hold dance competitions for the slaves, and watching those events was a favorite past-time. The winners were awarded a cake, giving rise to the expressions "takes the cake" and "a piece of cake." The dances, which were parodies of the European ballroom dances, involved a combination of African dance steps, high kicks, and exaggerated steps. One quite popular form was danced by a few couples, with their arms linked, lined up in a circle. They would dance forward, with alternate high kicks and short hops. Some say it originated from the "chalk-line walk" which was a rather simple dance performed by couples advancing on a straight line, balancing water buckets on the heads. The participants always wore flamboyant clothes and accessories, meant to amuse the spectators. As the music developed over the decades, it was often performed by a band or even a small orchestra, but it was always intended for dancing. The cakewalk in its original form was slightly syncopated, and even later was never as sophisticated as true ragtime music.

Ernest Hogan was the composer of the song "All Coons Look Alike to Me." When published in 1986, it was the first to have the word "rag" on the sheet music.

Sheet music of "The Cake-Walk In The Sky", a very popular song of the era.

Ragtime was played many years before it was first published in the late 1890s, but the first time the term appears is on the sheet music from 1896 for Ernest Hogan's song "All Coons Look Alike to Me," still spelled as two words. The form of one word started to appear around 1898.

No one knows the exact origin of the word, but an anecdotal story tells that Scott Joplin, the greatest ragtime composer (1868-1917) once told a reporter that it was named so "because it had such a ragged movement."

It is an established fact that the pianists at the Chicago World's Fair, in 1893, played this type of music. Ragtime is characterized by elaborately syncopated rhythm in the melody and a steadily accented accompaniment.

The accented left-hand beat is opposed in the right hand by a fast, bouncing melody that gave the music its powerful forward impetus.

Ragtime compositions typically featured three or four discrete 16-bar strains performed at a moderate tempo. The rhythm and structure of ragtime were important influences on the development of jazz.

Ernest Hogan's "All Coons Look Alike to Me" has an appendix that starts with the words "Choice Chorus, with Negro Rag; accompaniment, and arrangement by Max Hoffmann." The offensive title is somewhat misleading. In the song, the insulting words are said not by a white man who is looking down on blacks, but by a black woman who is explaining her attraction to a new boyfriend who had supplanted all other men in her heart, and she has no eyes for anyone else. The song sold extremely well not only as sheet music but as wax cylinders, but they were not reissued because of the racist implications. Nevertheless, the song was so popular that it was adopted by white singers as well as black ones.

Lyrics of the song: All Coons look alike to me

[Verse]

Talk about a coon a having trouble
I think I have enough of ma own
It's all about ma Lucy Janey Stubbles
And she has caused my heart to mourn
Thar's another coon barber from Virginia
In soci'ty he's the leader of the day
And now ma honey gal is gwine to quit me
Yes, she's gone and drove this coon [i.e., me] away
She's no excuse
To turn me loose
I've been abused
I'm all confused
'Cause these words she did say:

[CHORUS]

All coons look alike to me
I've got another beau, you see,
And he's just as good to me as you, nig! ever tried to be
He spends his money free,
I know we can't agree
So I don't like you no how
All coons look alike to me

*** *** ***

Ernest Hogan further developed the popularity of this type of music by creating the "Memphis Students", an all black orchestra, in 1905.
This orchestra was a novelty to white audiences, who greatly enjoyed the wild sight of the dancing conductor, the athletic jumping and hopping of the drummers, and the unusual choice of instruments, which included saxophones, guitars, banjos, and mandolins – instruments that were not employed in traditional orchestras. This was a most effective way to bring the syncopated music and the African-American artists into the limelight, and indeed, many songs written by African Americans sold extremely well: That's Why They Call me Shine (1910), by Ford Dabney, who also led an orchestra, Castle Walk (1914), by Vernon and

168

Irene Castle), Walkin' The Dog (1916) and Darktown Strutters Ball (1917), by Shelton Brooks, After You've Gone (1918), Strut Miss Lizzie (1921) and Way Down Yonder in New Orleans (1922), by John Turner Layton, among others.

Photos from L to R: 1-Bob Cole and Rosamond Johnson. Cole was born in Athens, Georgia, on July 1, 1868. 2-Tom Turpin, publisher of "Harlem Rag", a big hit of the era.

Cole's earliest published songs were issued in 1893, and one of his earliest stage jobs was with Sam T. Jack's Creole Show, the first African-American show to break from the strict minstrel tradition of all male performers. Cole also performed as an actor and directed the All Star Stock Company at Worth's Museum in New York, the first such company organized by African-Americans.

Ragtime: An important part of American culture.

Ragtime's highest popularity coincides with the career of its greatest, Scott Joplin. However, other than the "Maple Leaf Rag," ragtime went into obscurity, until its revival in the 1940, brought about by jazz enthusiasts who were researching the roots of jazz, brought it back into the light. In addition, the 1973 film, *The Sting*, used ragtime as the soundtrack.

However, there were many other contributors. "Mississippi Rag," written by the white composer William H. Krell was published in 1897, and is considered by some to be the first published rag, but in truth it is a march.

At the same year, an African-American composer, Tom Turpin, published "Harlem Rag," which enjoyed a great success. Interestingly, the most popular rag of the early twentieth century was also written by a white composer, Euday, L. Bowman, called "12th Street Rag" and published in 1914. It was recorded by several artists, including Louis Armstrong in 1914 and Pee Wee Hunt in 1948. Ragtime is still played, and recorded regularly, but it is basically limited to a small audience.

The "coon songs," are now distasteful to all of us due to their stereotypes and racial tones, but they cannot be ignored since they represented an important genre a century ago. One must remember that comic songs exist about every ethnic group, and keep the historical perspective. These songs sold very well, both as illustrated sheet music and records, by such large companies as Victor, Edison, and Columbia. Actually, some songs, even though not strictly "coon songs" were advertised as such, since it increased sales.

For example, when Billy Murray sang various comic songs for the Edison's National Phonograph Company, they promoted Irish songs like "Bedelia" and "Mary Ellen" as "Irish coon serenades!"

Interestingly, many people associated the coon songs with ragtime, even though the coon songs predated rag.

Some of the most important songs were:

- Whistling Coon
- You'll Have To Choose Another Baby Now
- My Coal Black Lady
- The Wench With The Rag Time Walk
- You've Been A Good Ole Wagon, But You're Done Broke Down
- I Love My Little Honey, is characterized as a "rag time melody."
- Bill Bailey, Won't You Please Come Home?

- Under the Bamboo Tree
- Good Bye, My Lady Love

Many of the songs included the words "ragtime" in the titles.

In 1900, ragtime meant "coon songs", not piano music; songs with comic words describing the lives and milieux of blacks and cakewalks. In 1910, ragtime meant vivacious orchestral dance music popular with young audiences. And quite often, composers and sheet music publishers would add the word "rag" to the songs to increase sales.

The word "rag" was very fashionable. Starting with 1919, the word "blues" became en vogue and replaced the word "rag". Today, music historians have the tendency to describe ragtime music as a musical piece played by a solo pianist, and refer to Scott Joplin as the pioneer of the genre.

Ironically, Scott Joplin's music was never recorded during his heyday, but he did cut minimal pianos rolls. The music industry, as well as the general public, preferred banjos and brass bands. Probably, this explains the popularity of bandleader Sousa and legendary banjoist Vess L. Ossman. Many white musicians tried to record ragtime music.

In fact, the first and earliest ragtime recording was done by a white pianist by the name of C. H. Booth on November 1, 1901.

And the first recorded ragtime song was "Creole Belles" written by J. Bodewalt Lempe. Around 1900-1901, march music and ragtime music were in demand. So, to increase the sales of the recently cut "Creole Belles", the publishers promoted the song as "Rag-time march."

The best ragtime piece of the era was "Maple Leaf Rag" written by Scott Joplin in 1899. Although it was recorded 8 times during his life time, no recordings of "Maple Leaf Rag" sold well. Joplin died in 1917.

The most popular songs of the era were:

- Harlem Rag, by Tom Turpin (1873 - 1922),
- Mississippi Rag (1897), by William H. Krell,
- Dusty Rag (1908) by May Aufderheide (1888 – 1972),
- Frog Legs Rag, by James Slyvester Scott (1885 - 1938),
- Wall Street Rag, by Scott Joplin,
- Gladiolus Rag, by Scott Joplin.

Tom Turpin

Tom Turpin was a musician and businessman whose bar in St. Louis became an important gathering place for ragtime musicians, including Scott Joplin. Turpin was born in Savannah, Georgia, and moved with his family to St. Louis in the early 1880s.

Turpin's father ran a saloon and was active in local politics. Together with his brother Charles, Turpin traveled west and invested in a Nevada gold mine. When this venture proved to be unsuccessful, Turpin returned to St. Louis and opened the Rosebud Bar at 2220 Market Street.

This saloon became a focal point for the ragtime music scene. Tom Turpin's own musical output was small compared to that of other ragtime composers.

He did, however, have a strong influence on the development of ragtime. In fact, his composition "The Harlem Rag" (1897) is considered the first published rag by an African American.

His other compositions include "The Harlem Rag" (1897), "The Bowery Buck" (1899), "A Ragtime Nightmare" (1900), "St. Louis Rag" (1903), "The Buffalo Rag" (1904), and "Pan-Am Rag" (1914). He is buried in St. Peter's Cemetery in St. Louis, Missouri.

*** *** ***

Cakewalks in the ragtime era

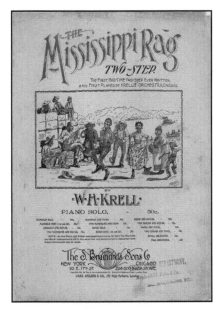

Photo: Mississippi Rag by William H. Krell. New York, New York, NY: S. Brainard's Sons, 1897.

First published composition with the word "cakewalk":

The first composition to be published with the word "cakewalk" in the title was "Opelika Cakewalk" in 1892, but it was "Rastus on Parade" that had really started the cakewalk craze in 1895. It also established the structure – the piece had to start in a minor key and end in a major key. Since both ragtime and cakewalk are syncopated, and emerged roughly the same time, considerable confusion exists in labeling them. In addition, greedy publishers, wishing to make a profit, sometimes mislabeled the pieces deliberately, depending which of the two forms was more saleable at the time. "Mississippi Rag," for instance, which was published in 1897, is actually a cakewalk.

To complicate things even further, sometimes the composers themselves were to blame. For example, Scott Joplin's "Swipesy Cakewalk" is really a rag! Even at the time, controversy over cakewalks never quite stopped.

The *Cleveland Gazette*, for example, printed an angry article in 1893, blaming the pastor for allowing the dance in his church, since it was a relic of slavery days. The craze spread to Canada, and such great songs were written there as "The Cake Winner," by G.W. Adams.

ACCORDING to our Circleville, O., correspondence, published elsewhere in this paper, the pastor of the A. M. E. church of that place so far forgot himself as to permit a "*cake walk*" to be held in the *church*. The presiding elder of that district and bishop, also, ought to have an interview with the pastor at once. "Cake walks" are disgraceful relics of slavery days and should not be tolerated for a moment in intelligent Afro-American *communities*, to say nothing of *churches*.

Source: Library of Congress and Cleveland Gazette, Article: Cakewalk, Volume: 1 , Issue Number: 18 , Page2, Date: 12/09/1893.

*** *** ***

All time favorites

At A Darktown Cakewalk. Charles Hale. Philadelphia, PA: Belmont Music Co., 1899.

175

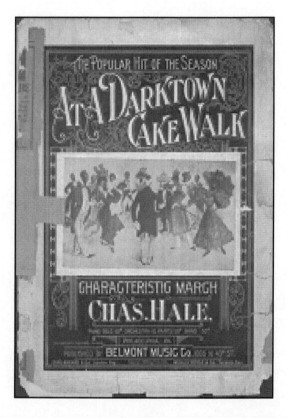

At A Georgia Camp Meeting: A Characteristic March Which Can be Used Effectively as a Two-Step Polka or Cake Walk. Kerry Mills. New York, NY: F.A. Mills, 1897.

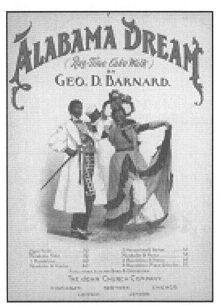

Photo from L to R: 1-Alabama Dream (Rag-Time Cake Walk). George D. Barnard. Cincinnati, OH: The John Church Company, 1899. 2-Aunt Hannah: March and Cake Walk. William Loraine. New York, NY: Hugo V. Schlam, 1900.

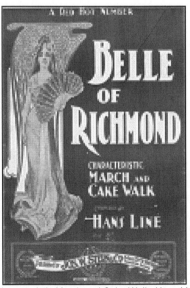

Belle of Richmond: Characteristic March and Cake Walk. Hans Liné. New York: Jos. W. Stern & Co., 1902.

The 50 most popular tunes
"Stick out your head"

Photo: A Galliker ice cream truck of the era. Ice cream trucks in towns throughout America played a version of "The Entertainer" through loudspeakers to attract customers and children.

That was the very first tune played by ice cream trucks in the United States.

Pastors in white neighborhoods did NOT allow white children to buy ice cream from trucks playing a "black tune". So owners of ice cream factories instructed the driver to "stick his head" out of the window, so everybody would see he was "white".

This is how, why, and when the expression "stick out your head" or "stick out your neck" entered the American vocabulary. It entered from the window of an ice cream truck.

List of the most popular songs

1-**After the Cakewalk.** Nathaniel Dett. Toronto, ON: Whaley, Royce & Co., 1900.

2-**Alabama Dream (Rag-Time Cake Walk).** George D. Barnard. Cincinnati, OH: The John Church Company, 1899.

3-**Alagazam! Cake Walk, March, and Two Step**. Abe Holzmann. NY, 1902.

4-**At A Darktown Cakewalk.** Charles Hale. Philadelphia, PA: Belmont Music Co., 1899.

5-**At A Georgia Camp Meeting: A Characteristic March Which Can be Used Effectively as a Two-Step Polka or**

6-**Cake Walk**. Kerry Mills. New York, NY: F.A. Mills, 1897.

7-**Audacious Arabella: Cake Walk March**. Hanna Rion. New York, NY: F.A. Mills, 1900.

8-**Aunt Hannah: March and Cake Walk**. William Loraine. New York, NY: Hugo V. Schlam, 1900.

9-**Aunt Mandy's Wedding: March & Cake Walk**. Wm. H. Tyers. New York, NY: Jos. W. Stern, 1899.

10-**Aunt Minervy Anns: Cake Walk and Characteristic March**. Joseph St. John. Montreal, QC: 1900.

11-**Bamboo Cake Walk.** C.G. McIntosh. Melbourne: Allan & Co., 1905.

12-**Belle of Richmond: Characteristic March and Cake Walk**. Hans Liné. New York: Jos. W. Stern & Co., 1902.

13-**Belle of the Cake Walk**: March. Lawrence B. O'Connor. Boston, MA: B.F. Wood Music Co., 1897.

14-**Black Cinderella Cake Walk**. Florence Wood. Toledo, OH: Peter McCormick, 1900.

15-**Blackville Society Cake Walk and Two Step**. Bernard Franklin. Boston, MA: G.W. Setchell, 1899.

16-**Bluffton Carnival Rag: Cake Walk**. Verdi Karns. Bluffton, IN: Verdi Karns, 1899.

17-**The Bos'n Rag: Cake Walk**. Fred S. Stone. Detroit, MI: Whitney Warner Pub. Co.,1899.

18-**The Brooklyn Cake Walk** (The Permans' Brooklyn Cake Walk). T.W. Thurban. Melbourne : Allan's, 1899.

19-**Bunch O' Blackberries: Cake - Walk & Two - Step**. Abe Holzmann. New York, NY: Feist & Frankenthaler, 1899.

20-**The Cake-Walk in the Sky**. Ben Harney. New York, NY: M. Witmark & Sons, 1899.

21-**The Cake Walk Patrol: Two Step**. W.H. Krell. Chicago, IL: The S. Brainard's Sons Co., 1895.

22-**The Cake Winner**. G.W. Adams. Toronto, ON: Amey & Hodgins, 1909.

23-**Car-Barlick-Acid Rag: Two-Step-Cake Walk**. Clarence C. Wiley. Detroit, MI: Jerome H. Remick & Co., 1905.

24-**Careless Sam: Cake Walk & Two Step**. John H. Davies. Kansas City, MO: J.W. Jenkins' Sons Music Company, 1900.

25-**Carolina Tar Heel Cake Walk**. Dan Sullivan. New York, NY: White-Smith Music Pub. Co.,1898.

26-**Chocolate Drops: A Darktown Improbability. Suitable for March, Cake Walk or Two Step**. Harry Von Tilzer., NY, 1902.

27-**Colored Aristocracy: Cake Walk**. Gus W. Bernard. Indianapolis, IN: D.H. Baldwin, 1899.
28-**The Colored Major: Characteristic March And Two**. Stephen R. Henry. New York, NY: The Lyceum Publishing Co., 1900.
29-**A Coon Band Contest: Jazz Fox-Trot**. Arthur Pryor. New York, NY: Emil Ascher, 1918.   30-
Coon Hollow Capers: Cake Walk & Two Step. Frank R. Gillis. New York, NY: Hugo V. Schlam, 1900.
31-**De Coontown Jubilee: Cake Walk: An African Ragtime Oddity**. Clarence L. Partee. Kansas City, MO.1897.
32-**Coontown Jubilee: Rag Time Cake Walk, March and Two Step**. Leo Friedman. Chicago, IL: Sol Bloom, 1898.
33-**Coon-ville Festival Cakewalk**. Gus H. Kline. Chicago, IL: G.H. Kline, 1898.
34-**The Cotton Pickers: Characteristic Rag Time, Two Step or Cake Walk**. Will Hardy. Haverhill, MA, 1899.
35-**Cotton Pickers Rag: Original Cake Walk**. Wm. J. Braun. New Orleans, LA: Louis Grunewald Co. Ltd., 1899.
36-**Creole Belles: March-Two-Step**. J. Bodewalt Lampe. Detroit, MI: Whitney-Warner Publishing Co., 1900.
37-**Cuban Cake Walk**. James T. Brymn. New York, NY: Richard A. Saalfield, 1901.
38-**Dandy Dan: Two-Step & Cake-Walk**. Julian Fredericks. New York, NY: Jos. W. Stern & Co., 1909.
39-**The Darkies Delight: Two Step and Cakewalk**. Samuel Lapin. Springfield, MA: A.H. Goetting, 1899.
40-**The Darkie's Drill: Cake Walk**. Agnes Melville. Boston, MA: Avon Music Company, 1902.
41-**Darktown Excitement: March and Cake Walk**. William Brown. Baltimore, MD: George Willig & Co., 1900.
42-**Darktown Is Out To-Night: A Senegambian Review. March Two-Step**. Will Marion. New York, NY, 1899.
43-**Democratic Fun: A Campaign Cake-Walk**. Robert Buechel. Denver, CO: Tolbert R. Ingram Music Co., 1908.
44-**Dixie Flyer: Cakewalk and Two Step**. A.E. Henrich. Mt. Vernon, IN: A.E. Henrich, 1901.
45-**Doc Brown's Cake Walk:** Kansas City Rag. Charles L. Johnson. Kansas City, MO: J.W. Jenkins' Sons, 1899.
46-**Down on The Old Plantation:** Cake-Walk. Bayard Wilson. Philadelphia, PA: M. D. Swisher, 1899.

47-**Dusky Dinah:** Cake-walk and Patrol. Dan J. Sullivan. Boston, MA: Chas. Shackford 1899.
48-**Dusky Dudes**. Jean Schwartz (lyrics by Will. A. Heelan). New York, NY: Shapiro, Bernstein & Von Tilzer, 1899.
49-**Give Cinda the Cake**: March and Two Step. Theo A. Metz. New York, NY: Edward Schuberth & Co., 1898.
50-**Good Enough!** Rollin Howard. Chicago, IL: Lyon & Healy, 1871.

***   ***   ***

Aunt Mandy's Wedding: **March & Cake Walk**. Wm. H. Tyers. New York, NY: Jos. W. Stern, 1899.

Ragtime women composers

Photo: Sheet music for The Tanguay Tangle. Lyrics by Merrill, Blanche.
Music by Leo Edwards. Singer: Eva Tanguay. Publisher: Charles K.
Harris, 1912. New York.

The Work of Early Female Songwriters:

Sometimes, it was extremely difficult to know whether the
musical work was done by a man or a woman, because female
composers and singers –in many instances- were NOT allowed to
use their full names. Only their initials were printed on the music
sheet!! Ironically, this prejudice and bias against women reminds
me of the early days of Greek theater, when women were not
allowed to appear or perform on stage.
So male performers had to disguise themselves as women. C'est
la vie! But fortunately "la vie" has changed.

Today, the most successful recording artists are women, and their names shine wide and bright in light!

Famous Female Composers:
The greatest ragtime composers of the era were: Scott Joplin, Joseph F. Lamb and James Scott.

However, one woman in particular, May Irwin did rival the quality of those three giants. Despite the fact that ragtime music rotated around a "male world" fueled by solo male pianists, and men gambling in smoke-filled saloons, women were avid consumers of ragtime sheet music.

And some became famous composers of the genre, to name a few:

- Abbie Ford
- Adaline Shepherd
- Alma M. Sanders
- Anita Comfort
- Anita Owen
- Bess E. Rudisill
- Blanche M. Tice
- Carlotta Williamson
- Charlotte Blake
- Fleta Jan Brown
- Florence McPherran
- Grace LeBoy
- Hattie Starr
- Henrietta B. Blanke (Belcher)
- Irene Cozad
- Irene Giblin
- Julia L. Niebergall
- Libbie Erickson
- Louise Gustin
- Luella Lockwood Moore
- Mabel McKinley
- Mamie E. Williams
- Marie Louka
- Maude Nugent
- May Aufderheide
- Muriel Pollock
- Nellie M. Stokes
- Nellie Weldon Cocroft
- Pauline B. Story
- Sadie Koninsky
- Verdi Karns

Chapter 10
The fabulous soloists of the golden era of the brass bands

***   ***   ***

Chapter 10
The fabulous soloists of the golden era of the brass bands

The most famous bandleaders in the late nineteenth century, from left to right:
1-Patrick Gilmore, an Irish-born composer who wrote the lyrics to the song "When Johnny Comes Marching Home", originally "Johnny I Hardly Knew Ye", an old Irish antiwar folk song,
2-John Philip Sousa is best remembered for his glorious marches and spectacular band. Sousa wrote 136 marches, including *The Stars and Stripes Forever*, the national march of the United States. The march's official premiere was in Philadelphia on May 14, 1897.
3-Alessandro Liberati.

4-Arthur Pryor was the very first bandleader to record a musical work. Before creating his own band, Pryor was the trombone soloist of John Phillip Sousa band.
5-Patrick Conway. At fifteen, and following the death of his father, Conway went to work at a carriage factory, where a fellow worker taught him how to play the cornet. In 1895 Conway moved to Ithaca to teach music at Cornell.
6-Edwin Franko Goldman had the solo chair in the Metropolitan Opera Orchestra.

Historically and originally, the march as a musical form was associated mostly with the military, but later on, it became dancers' favored choice, because the regular rhythm in 2/4, 4/4, or 6/8 meter was perfect for the extremely popular Fox-Trot. March music was in demand. Sousa's famous marches were written for every musical instrument, including piano, banjo, flute and mandolin.

Brass bands music was heard everywhere in America, and was widely used in weddings, parties, official parades, concert halls, receptions and ice skating parks. Colleges, universities and towns in America raised funds to support marching bands. In 1889, Leon Mead wrote in the Harper's Weekly: "At present there are over ten thousand military bands in the United States. In the smaller cities they average twenty-five men each. In small county towns they number twelve to eighteen members." Brass bands and marching bands played all sorts of music including opera, ragtime, popular tunes, and melodies such as "Yankee Doodle" and "The Carnival of Venice".

The era's most famous solo musicians:

The era's most famous solo musicians, referred to as instrumentalists, and America's first recording stars-artists were: Alice Raymond called the "World's Greatest Lady Cornetist", Walter B. Rogers, Jules Levy, the most celebrated cornet player of his time; Cornet player, Herbert L. Clarke from the Sousa Band, Emil Keneke, and Bohumir Kryl, a cornetist virtuoso from Bohemia. Despite their enormous popularity, those artists did not sell enough records, because in 1890s, few Americans homes could afford equipment for playing records. Sousa was the biggest star of the era.

The Fabulous Soloists:

Huge crowds in the thousands would gather for public concerts given by brass bands. The highlights of those festive events were the soloists. They were the superstars of the concerts. Famous trombonists, cornetists, and horn players were the toast of the town. And some became extremely wealthy.

For instance, the legendary Jules Levy, earned more than $10,000 per year; a fortune in those days.

The soloists were virtuosi, immensely creative and musical acrobats! Each one had his own style and specialized in dazzling techniques such as intervallic leaps, flying fingers, and triple tonguing. And the adoring public nicknamed each one of them according to his technique and dazzling style. Soloists were given glorious names and titles, such as "The King of the Cornet", "The World Greatest Horn Maestro", "The Greatest Cornetist", "The Golden Fingers", you name it!

Among the greatest soloists of the era were:
- From France: Saint Jacome, Henry Maury and Jean Baptiste Arban.
- From Germany: Hermann Bellstedt and Theodor Hoch.
- From Italy: Allesandro Liberati.
- From the United Kingdom: Jack Macintosh, John Hartmann, and George Swift.
- From Bohemia: Bohumir Kryl.
- From the United States: Frank Holton, Leo Zimmerman, Arthur Pryor, Henry Filmore, Walter M. Smith, Del Staigers, Herbert Clarke, Framk Simon, Walter Rogers, Ben Bent, Walter Emerson, and W. Paris Chambers.
- From Scotland: Mathew Arbuckle.

Other great brass soloists included also Thomas D. van Osten, Somone Mantia, and Joseph DeLuca.

The Great Musicians of the Era:

1-Bohumir Kryl (1875-1961). A celebrated cornet player, born in Bohemia, Kryl immigrated to the United States in 1889. Kryl first became known as soloist virtuoso for the John Phillip Sousa band.

Later he joined Frederick N. Innes' band, and became its assistant director.

After a few years, Kryl decided to create his own band, and his success was legendary.

His playing was compared to Caruso's singing! His range and tone were astonishing. He was the first solo instrumentalist who produced multiphonics on a cornet referred to as the "different tone"; an innovative cornet technique consisting of playing a low pitch while humming a higher pitch, thus producing a third pitch. This very third pich was called "the different tone"and was louder than both, the note

189

or the hum. No cornet or trumpet player of the era could reach his range or duplicate his tone.

2- Herbert Lincoln Clarke (1867-1945) acknowledged to be the greatest cornetist of his time, was certainly the most celebrated.

Not only was he a virtuoso cornet player, but "an excellent composer, an accomplished violinist, a prolific and highly talented arranger for band, and a most distinguished band conductor" (Johnston, Jan. 1972, p. 44).

As well, he wrote several study books for the cornet that are still used today.

Clarke was born in Woburn, Massachusetts on September 12, 1867. He moved with his family to Toronto in 1880.

Since his father was the organist at the Jarvis St. Baptist Church and his three older brothers played with the Regimental Band of the Queen's Own Rifles, it was not surprising that the young Clarke showed an interest in music. He himself said in his autobiography, *How I Became a Cornetist*, that it was growing up "in a musical environment that played a large part in turning me to the musically artistic as a life profession".

In the spring of 1881 he attended a concert of The American Band of Providence, Rhode Island, at the Horticultural Pavilion in Toronto and he heard Bowen R. Church play a cornet solo. Later, Clarke was to remember this event as the most significant of his childhood. He taught himself to play the cornet, using his brother Edwin's instrument. At about the same time, he joined the Toronto Philharmonic Orchestra, conducted by Dr. F. H. Torrington, as a violinist.

The cornet had captured his heart, however. In 1882, he joined the Queen's Own Rifles band as the last chair of a 12-man cornet section in order to obtain a government-issue instrument on which to practise. Between 1884, when he graduated from high school, and 1887, Clarke drifted between playing in the pit orchestra of English's Opera House in Indianapolis, where his family had moved; working (unhappily) at the John Kay store in Toronto, while playing second chair cornetist with the Queen's Own; and playing at the Ontario Beach lake resort in the summer. It was in 1887 that he joined the Citizen's Band of Toronto, under John Bayley, as the band's cornet soloist.

He spent the next five years playing in and leading several bands around Toronto (the Taylor Safe Works Band, Heintzman Piano Company Band, Streetsville Ontario Band) and teaching at the Toronto Conservatory of Music (where he also played in the Toronto Conservatory String Quartet) and at Trinity College in Port Hope, Ontario.

In September of 1889 he married Elizabeth (Lizzie) Loudon, with whom he had two children: Vivian (Grace) in 1890 and James (Edward James Watkin) in 1892.

In the spring of 1892, he left Canada once again, after successfully auditioning for the Gilmore Band. In 1893, he joined Sousa's Band as a cornet soloist.

After playing at the Chicago Exposition in the same year, he left to play with various other bands, continuing to do so over the next five years. It was during this period that he divorced Lizzie Loudon and married Lillian Bell Hause, with whom he had two more children, Ruby Bell and Herbert L. Clarke, Jr. In 1898 he returned to Sousa's Band, with whom he toured extensively, and later became Sousa's assistant director, conducting the band in many recording sessions. He resigned from Sousa's band in September of 1917 and returned to Canada to lead the Anglo-Canadian Leather Company Band in Huntsville, Ontario from 1918 to 1923.

Under Clarke's leadership, this band became one of the most celebrated commercial bands in North America. In 1923, he moved to Long Beach, California due to his wife's health and conducted the Long Beach Municipal Band until 1943. In April of 1934, he was elected President of the American Bandmasters Association. He died in January 1945 and his ashes were interred at the Congressional Cemetery in Washington, D.C., near the gravesite of John Phillip Sousa.

His papers and memorabilia are held at The Sousa Archives and Center for American Music at the University of Illinois at Urbana-Champaign. In the course of his musical career, Clarke recorded most of his own solo cornet compositions, other cornet solos and conducted Sousa's Band in over 200 recordings. Among his recordings were "Bride of the Waves", "Sounds from the Hudson" and "Caprice Brilliante", as a soloist; "Hunting Scene", conducting the American Band of Providence; and "The Stars and Stripes Forever", "Semper Fidelis" and "Favourite Songs of Canada", conducting Sousa's Band.

Several of his recordings were reissued on Crystal Records disc S450 around 1979. A discography can be found in Roll Back the Years. (Data: Collections Canada)

3-John Hazel (1865-1948). When Hazel performed for the first time as a guest soloist with Patrick Gilmore's 22nd Regiment Band in New York City, a prominent national music critic dubbed him "one of the greatest cornetists the world has ever produced."

His success was spectacular, and he recorded hundreds of tunes -solos and duets -with the Edison Studio band. In addition, he recorded more than 300 tunes for the Edison Phonographic Studios.

Known as the "Wizard Cornetist" in an era when concerts in the park were as popular as rock concerts are today and community bands numbered in the tens of thousands, John Hazel returned to Williamsport, Pennsylvania in 1907 upon his retirement as a performer and lent his considerable musical expertise to local musical activities.

Hazel was born in Bellefonte, Pennsylvania in September 28, 1865 and died in Williamsport in January 26, 1948. In 1891, he was a guest soloist with Patrick Gilmore's famed 22nd Regiment Band in New York City.

Soon a national music magazine of the time hailed him as "one of the greatest cornetists the world has produced." From 1903 to 1907, Hazel was invited to record several solos and duets for the Edison Phonographic Studios.

In addition, he also performed on hundreds of records with the Edison studio band and orchestra.

192

He wrote and arranged numerous compositions for performance by the Repasz Band. Some of his most famous marches are still performed today.

In 1995, the Repasz Band and Williamsport's Scottish Rite Imperial Teteque Band featured a guest trumpet soloist, Dr. Mark Murray, as a fund raising effort to provide a permanent interactive exhibit dedicated to John Hazel at the Lycoming County Historical Society's Museum in Williamsport. (Journal of the Lycoming County Historical Society)

4-Rafael Mendez (1906-1981) was born in Jiqulpan, Mexico. He was a virtuoso and flamboyant trumpet player with a dashing style. At the age of five, he joined the family orchestra, which became extremely popular upon joining Pancho Villa, who loved the music of the Méndez, and kept them in his service for five years.

In 1921, Rafael Méndez joined the Mexican army and became member of the army orchestra.

At age 20, he moved to the United States, and after a short time, he joined the MGM orchestra, and played in various movies until 1949. In 1950, Méndez recorded 45 tunes for Decca records. In 1952, he began to tour the United States and Europe.

5-Claude Gordon (1916-1996) at the age of eight, played as a soloist trumpeter with the Helena Montana High School Band.

He studied with Louis Maggio and the legendary Herbert L. Clarke. He got his first gig with the CBS studios orchestra in Los Angeles.

A few years later, Gordon began to play for NBC radio, and on many TV shows and specials.

In 1959, he created his own orchestra and was dubbed the "Best New Band in America."

In addition to conducting and writing scores, Gordon also wrote training books and taught in colleges and private studios.

6-Jules Levy (1839-1903) was the most celebrated cornetist of the era. He led the legendary Gilmore Band. In 1883, in recognition for his remarkable services to the music industry, Levy was given a diamond studded cornet, built by C.G. Conn Company.

In 1878, Levy became the first musician to make test recordings for Edison.

Levy made twenty three recordings for Victor Records, and fifteen for Columbia.

7-Paul Staigers (1899-1950). When he played his first solo at Winona Lake, Indiana Chautauqua, Staigers was dubbed "The Boy Wonder."

He began his career at an early age with the NHDVS Band in Dayton, Ohio.

In March of 1918, Sousa hired him as the assistant cornet soloist to Frank Simon, responsible for the Willow Grove Concerts.

In 1926, Edwin Franko Goldman offered him a better deal and hired him as soloist.

Staigers stayed with the band until 1934.

He continued to perform in major events, and to teach in New York until he moved in 1943 to Los Angeles, where he worked for the radio and film industry.

8-Meredith Wilson (1902–1984). A flute and piccolo player, Wilson is best known for the writing the best-seller "The Music Man"; a touching story of a band instrument salesman who went to a small town in Iowa, and changed the

194

town forever. Wilson also wrote musical scores for a great number of motion pictures. He played for John Philip Sousa's band from 1921 to 1923, and in the New York Philharmonic Orchestra from 1924 to 1929, when the great Arturo Toscanini was its conductor.

In 1931, Willson moved to San Francisco, California to take on the position of concert director for KFRC. A few years later, he became the musical director of the NBC radio network in Hollywood.

9-Herman Bellstedt came to America in 1867 at the age of nine.

His family settled in Cincinnati in 1872 where he studied the cornet with his father and Mylius Weigand.

Being billed as the "Boy Wonder" he gave his debut performance on 10 May 1873. He then performed second cornet in the orchestra at Arctic Gardens, soon being promoted to first cornet and soloist.

In 1874, he performed solo cornet with the Cincinnati Reed Band for five years under the direction of Michael Brand. In 1879, he became cornet soloist with the Red Hussar Band on Manhattan Beach, later returning to the Cincinnati Reed Band in 1883.

He performed from 1889 to 1892 in Gilmore's Band sitting next to Benjamin Bent, from 1904 to 1906 in Sousa's Band (replacing Walter B. Rogers) performing next to Herbert L. Clarke, and from 1906 to 1909 in Frederick N. Innes' Band (replacing Bohumir Kryl).

He was billed by Innes as "Germany's Greatest Cornet Soloist" (Schwartz 1957, 235-6). Bellstedt's talents extended well beyond the cornet realm, as he conducted the Bellstedt & Ballenberg Band and performed first trumpet in orchestras conducted by Theodore Thomas, Van der Stucken, and Schradieck between the years of 1892 and 1904. (Medina Community Band)

10-Mathew Arbuckle (1828-1883) was one of Patrick Gilmore's greatest cornet soloists. Matthew Arbuckle was born in Lochside, near Glasgow, Scotland 1828, into a very musical family.

195

His father was an excellent violinist, his mother a fine vocalist. At the age of 13 he persuaded his father to let him enter the English Army as a musician.

He joined the band of the 26th Cameriorians, serving with them during the "Opium War" with China and the "Sikh War" in India. When he came back to England he started studying music, and developing his skills. He studied cornet in London with Herman Koenig).

Even if Arbuckle soon was one of the best cornet players in the Army, he realised that this was not the best place for a soloist.

He took what is called a "French leave" - in other words he deserted the Army. (This is also why he never came back to England on tour).

In 1853 he came to Canada. He was a bagpiper and drum major with the Royal Scottish Regiment of Canada, as well as cornet soloist. In 1857 he became a member of the Troy Brass Band in New York. A warm summer's day in 1857 in New York, Isaac Fiske) saw and heard Arbuckle play with the Troy Band and was very impressed. He persuaded Arbuckle to join Fiske's Cornet Band of Worcester (which used Fiske instruments only). When Fiske went back to Worcester the next day, Matthew Arbuckle accompanied him. Arbuckle remained in Worcester for three years marching at the head of Fiske's band in the finest uniform Isaac Fiske could buy.

The famous Gilmore Band visited Worcester in 1860 and Arbuckle put on such a show that Patrick Gilmore felt he had to have him for his band. In spite of a lawsuit by Fiske, Matthew Arbuckle joined Gilmore's Band. Arbuckle played solo cornet at the National Peace Jubilee) of 1869 and the World Peace Jubilee of 1872, both held in Boston and organized by Patrick S. Gilmore.

At the National Peace Jubilee in 1869, Arbuckle played the trumpet obbligato, accompanying Madame Parepa Rosa in the famous aria from Samson by G. F. Handel, "Let the Bright Seraphim".

At the World Peace Jubilee of 1872, Arbuckle conducted the opening fanfare of fifty trumpeters and played the same trumpet obbligato part with Madame Ermina Ruggersdorf. In 1880, he became the musical director and bandmaster for the Ninth Regiment in New York. He held this position until his death. Matthew Arbuckle died suddenly in New York, 23 May 1883, at the age of 55. (Data: Abel Hive)

Karl King at the time he was appointed director of the Fort Dodge Municipal Band

11-Karl King's gift for composing was apparent at an early age, and he had several compositions published while still in his teens. In all, King published over 200 marches.

In addition to this impressive feat, which earned him the title *America's March King*, he also composed waltzes, overtures, intermezzos, serenades, dirges, rags, and galops, totaling almost another 100 selections.

Karl King moved to Fort Dodge, Iowa, in 1920 as the result of a classified advertisement in a national musician's publication for the position of conductor of the Fort Dodge Municipal Band, a post which he accepted and held for over 50 years. There in Fort Dodge he raised his family (one son, Karl Jr.), established a successful music publishing business, composed music, and directed the municipal band. He and his band appeared at numerous state and regional fairs, rodeos and expositions, as well as local concerts. The official title of the band was the Fort Dodge Municipal Band, but within a short time after he assumed leadership of the group it became known simply as King's Band. After his death, it was formally renamed the Karl L. King Municipal Band of Fort Dodge. (Source: Medina Community Band)

Note:
Sousa saw "recorded music" as a threat to the livelihood of musicians
Sousa recorded over 1,000 tunes, even though, he publicly showed disdain for "mechanical music", a term he used to describe "music recording". Sousa was the first recording artist to nickname recorded music as "canned music." In the September 1906 issue of the Appleton Magazine, Sousa wrote: "Canned music is as incongruous by a campfire as canned salmon by a trout stream." And the headline of the article was "The Menace of Mechanical Music!" Sousa was very concerned with professional musicians' livelihood. He feared that recorded music could and would replace musicians, and reduces live performances. Very true, Sousa was convinced that mechanical music (records and automated player pianos) were a real threat to musicians.

Photo: The Besses O' Th' Barn Band in 1900.

The golden age of the brass bands

Origin of the brass band.

Originally and historically, the brass band came to life in the early 19th century. England's industrial revolution was its cradle; an outgrowth of the medieval waits. Tycoons and powerful employers began to support and finance work bands in order to divert their employees preoccupation with steamy political activities which affected the flow of business, and employees productivity. Thus, brass bands were created and strongly encouraged in urban cities. The most visible bands of the era were:
- The Bessies O'Th Barn Brass Band and
- The Black Dyke Mills Brass Band.

In 1860, the United Kingdom had 755 brass bands.
Some were large and quite sophisticated for their time. Leading bands included a large section of trombones, flugelhorn, tenor horns, baritones, cornets, B flat and E flat basse, multiple drums and percussion.
At the beginning, the idea was created by businessmen and rich employers, but later on, politicians began to hire brass bands in their political campaigns. And in no time, corporations, groups and nonprofit organizations joined in.

Photo: A contemporary brass band in New Orleans, Louisiana.

The European Influence:

Immigrants from Italy, Ireland, Poland and Germany and other countries strongly influenced the American way of life, music and popular culture in the 1850s.

In 1840, Francis Scala, a virtuoso on the E-flat clarinet who imigrated from Napoli, Italy became the leader of the U.S. Marine Band, and incorporated the woodwinds in the navy band, and transformed the clarinet into the major instrument of all his bands.

He did encourage brasswind solos, but the E-flat clarinet dominated the performances. In 1859, Patrick Sarsfield Gilmore, who emigrated from Ireland, added reeds to his brass band, and intensely used clarinets and piccolos to double the soprano brasses.

Patrick Gilmore was the first musical arranger in America to write arrangements and develop innovative instrumentation enabling a wind section to produce grandiose and full sound effects of a very large orchestra.

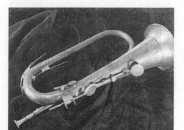

Photo: The B-flat and high E-flat keyed bugle was the most popular solo sound in the brass band.

The Germania Serenade Band, Jenny Lind and P.T. Barnum.

Photos: From L to R: 1-The Germania Serenade Band. 2-Entertainment promoter extraordinaire, P.T Barnum was a major driving force behind the establishment and development of brass bands in the United States. He used them everywhere.

The Germania Serenade band introduced the East Coast of America to the classics of Mozart, Beethoven, and other composers in the 1850s. With the great improvements of brass instruments, composers such as Berlioz, Meyerbeer, and later Franck, Wagner, and Verdi began to write beautiful solo passages for brass.

All members of the Germania Serenade Band, who have escaped religious persecution in Europe in 1848, introduced the East Coast of America to the classics of Mozart, Beethoven, and other composers in the 1850s. P. T. Barnum hired the Germania Serenade Band to accompany the "Swedish Nightingale," Jenny Lind, on her tour of the United States.

*** *** ***

Soprano Jenny Lind

Soprano Jenny Lind was born to an impoverished mother and a deadbeat dad. She became Europe's most famous female singer of the 19th century, in her early 20s. She toured Europe with composer Felix Mendelssohn. People, fans and admirers mobbed her concerts.

Soprano Jenny Lind.

She was a Victorian version of the Beatles. Jenny Lind turned down the marriage proposal of Hans Christian Anderson, the legendary children books author who furiously penned "The Ugly Duckling" in her honor. Lind time fell in love with Mendelssohn, but Helas, he was married. In 1850, entertainment promoter P.T Barnum brought Jenny Lind to the United States. She performed in more than 100 concerts with brass bands. P. T. Barnum engaged the Germania Serenade Brass Band to accompany Lind the "Swedish Nightingale" on her tour of the United States.

***   ***   ***

Chapter 11
An Old New Era

An Old New Era
The music was real musical composition, no Rap, heavy metal
and distorting noises.

At the beginning, music was real music.

Artists, performers, entertainers, musicians, composers and singers of yesteryears and at the dawn of American music were so different from those who came to the scene of the modern American music in the late 20th and early 21st centuries.

The music was real musical composition, no Rap, heavy metal and distorting noises. The lyrics were simple, evocative, poetic and polite and consequently, songs could be sung by all generations and audiences of all ages.

The musical productions were either super extravaganzas or daringly intimate and sentimental. The outfits, suits, dresses and wardrobes were either outrageous in their couture and style or traditionally elegant with refined cuts and elegant couture.

The make-up was extremely exaggerated, accentuated or theatrical.

The audience was strictly divided into two classes; the titled and entitled as one group, and the "tiers d'etat" as a second group. Some female artists made it big time.

Some earned a fortune while others despite their enormous success and superior artistic quality died in absolute poverty. Female artists did not know how to invest their money.

In many instances, they were used and misused, mistreated and taken advantage of by greedy impresarios, managers and agents. Success was based upon artistic quality, not fame and shame.

In brief, it was a different world. Folks around the turn of the century were singing *I Wonder Who's Kissing Her Now,* and others went for *When the Red, Red Robin Comes Bob, Bob, Bobing Along":*

When the red red Robin comes bob-bob-bobbing along, along.
There'll be no more sobbing when he starts throbbing his old sweet song.
Wake up, wake up you sleepy head,
Get up, get up get out of bed,
Cheer up cheer up the sun is red,
Live, love, laugh and be happy.
What if I've been blue, now I'm walking though fields of flowers.
Rain may glisten but still I listen for hours and hours.
I'm just a kid again doing what I did again singing a song.
When the red red Robin comes bob-bob-bobbing along, along."

Photo: Good old days of Vaudeville. Garland with cast members in Vaudeville review of 1932.

The good old days:

This was the beginning of the good times for American music, composers and singers.

It was a sweet and innocent time. The lyrics were simple and polite. The music was music and the song publishers on 28th Street between Sixth Avenue and Broadway in New York City were busy. Yes sir! This was the beginning of the good times for American music, composers and singers.

It was exciting for everybody; I can see Irving Berlin working on a new show, the extravagant Florenz Ziegfeld auditioning his female dancers and singers for his follies, ballroom dancing taking off, musicals on Broadway are in full gear, and cheap grotesque burlesque's joints are steaming.

Photo: Vaudeville show exhibit panel in 1920.

Vaudeville is booming and zooming, motion pictures are rolling, gramophones soaring, and cartoons, the latest novelty of the day are amusing and confusing many.

The world's first Cabaret "Le Chat Noir" which opened its doors for the first time in the Montmartre district of Paris in March 1881 gets a face lift.

It became the perfect place for adventurers, hustlers, raconteurs, drunken philosophers, poets, artists, composers and celebrities of the day such as Guy de Maupassant, Satie and de Debussy. The twentieth century is knocking at our doors; Broadway is in full swing with musicals and flashy dashy productions.

Two big productions take New York City by storm; "The Wizard of Oz".

The original draft of "Over the Rainbow" written before the story was not even completed.

Now, it is re-written again for the second time.

Considered cynical, the original draft will not see the light, and would be deleted from the original script, cut from the premiere and all the productions to follow.

Photo: Florenz Ziegfeld, America's first extravaganza entrepreneur extraordinaire.

Peter Pan

The play which made waves, was "Peter Pan". The two big hits of the era were "Give My Regards to Broadway" and "Meet me in St. Louis." Afro-Americans begin to sing the Blues in the fields and many Blues songs are recorded by talent scouts. Bessie Smith becomes the greatest Blues singer in the country. Harlem is still a white middle and upper-middle class community neighborhood of uptown Manhattan but, things are going to change now.

*** *** ***

Photo: Mary Martin. (1913-1990). Signed Early Photograph in her most famous role, "Peter Pan", with a charming inscription: "To Dawn Marie Slanter, the dearest little pot holder maker in all the world, with grateful thanks and affectionate greetings." The incomparable singer/actress originated the roles of Nellie in South Pacific and of Maria in The Sound of Music and won the NY Film Critics Circle Award in 1943 for One Touch of Venus. In 1955 and 1956, she received, first, a Tony Award for Peter Pan (Jerome Robbins), and then an Emmy Award for her appearance in the same role on television.

Bessie Smith

The Blues is born.

Philip Payton's Afro-Am Realty Company begins to lease and rent many of Harlem apartments and houses to black tenants around 135th Street East of Eighth Avenue and Harlem's. Blues expands East-West from Park to Amsterdam Avenue and North-South from 155th Street to Central Park.
The Blues is born. Soon, the Blues will invade the whole country and metamorphose into:

- Harlem Blues,
- Chicago Blues,
- California Blues,
- Country Blues,
- Louisiana Blues,
- Delta Blues,
- Bourbon Street Blues,
- Memphis Blues,
- Piedmont Blues,
- St. Louis Blues,
- Texas Blues,
- Urban Blues.

Simultaneously, Jazz begins to see the light, and mainly in New Orleans.
Jazz pioneers, such as Louis Armstrong, Jelly Roll Morton, and later Duke Ellington create new jazz tunes and compositions for big bands nightclubs and cabarets shows.
Jazz becomes a dominant force in the mainstream of American nightlife music thanks to creative and passionate singers, arrangers, composers and musicians such as, to name a few:

- Henry Allen,
- Lil Hardin-Armstrong,
- Albert Ammons,
- Eva Taylor,
- Mary Lou Williams,
- Nick LaRocca,
- Julia Lee,
- Billie Holiday,
- Lovie Austin,
- Mutt Carey,
- Elmer Snowden,
- Doc Cooke,
- Tiny Parham,
- Joseph Petit,
- Eddie Condon,
- Wrskine Tate,
- Lester Young,
- Clarence Williams,
- Sister Rosetta Tharpe,
- Ben Webster,

- Eddie Durham,
- Paul Whiteman,
- Jimmy Lunceford,
- Johnny Dunn,
- Milt Hinton,
- Fats Walle,
- Buster Bailey,
- Jimmy Dorsey,
- Benny Carter,
- Perry Bradford,
- Buddy Bolden,
- Cab Calloway,
- Tommy Dorsey,
- Harland Leonard,
- Jimmy Blythe,
- Sidney Bechet,
- Count Bassie,
- Benny Goodman,
- Earl Hines,
- Ben Pollack,
- Alphonse Picou,
- Mamie Smith,
- Willie "The Lion" Smith,
- Frank Trumbauer,
- Jack Teagarden.

Julia Lee

Mamie Smith

Eva Taylor

Mary Lou Williams

World War I: Change of time
New kind of music and lyrics

The music that got us through World War Two was very varied; stirring, romantic, sad, and comic. Much of the music was almost never to be played again, e.g. "There'll Be A Hot Time In Ol' Berlin," or "Praise The Lord And Pass The Ammunition." The two iconic songs of that dark period on this side of the Atlantic, at least, were sung by Jo Stafford ("I'll Be Seeing You") and Doris Day with Les Brown's band ("Sentimental Journey"). In Britain, Vera Lynn inspired the country with such songs as "The White Cliffs Of Dover" and "When The Lights Go On Again All Over The World." Plus, Glenn Miller's band had us swinging with "In The Mood." (Source: Examiner)

Jo Stafford was a super star!!

Music and lyrics begin to change in virtue of social changes caused by World War One.

Such changes were reflected in famous and popular songs of the era such as "Castle House Rag" and "On Patrol In No Man's Land" and "All Of No Man's Land Is Ours" recorded in March 1919, and performed by Noble Sissle, Henry Burr, Irving Kaufman, Billy Murray and Nora Bayes.

Other popular songs were "If You Were the Only Girl in the World", "Keep the Home Fires Burning", "Hinky Dinky Parlay Voo", "How Ya Gonna Keep 'em Down on the Farm" and particularly "I'm Always Chasing Rainbows".

And now, Irving Berlin steps in with a wave of fantastic songs such as "There's No Business Like Show Business", "White Christmas," and "God Bless America".

Eubie Blake and Noble Sissle.

Dinners with extravagant shows and musical acts.

Trendy restaurants and cafes like Palais Royal, Reisenweber, New York's Delmonico's and Shanley began to serve dinner with extravagant shows and musical acts.

Those early "boites" (Nightspots) came to be known as "cabarets" in the years before World War One, and short after, to be wiped out by the Prohibition.

Only a few glamorous and ritzy nightspots like the Cotton Club will continue to prosper after the ban on alcohol was lifted.

The "Speakeasies", a cabaret mobster-style began to spread nationwide.

At first they operated from backrooms and basements.
They called themselves "Clubs". It was a risky business, for the police constantly raided on them. Club' managers and their clienteles had to be careful. So, those colorful managers came up with a clever idea; all you had to do was to knock at the tiny door of the joint and tell the doorman "Joe sent me".
To attract more customers, the joints began to offer nightly live entertainment and musical acts. And of course, singing and performing on stage made things look legitimate.
Very soon after, cabarets and clubs owners discovered that women in the genre of "Femme Fatale" who sung romantically sad songs increased the sales of drinks and heavy alcohol. Live entertainment was a magical stroke.

*** *** ***

Singing women, "Saloon Singers" are the major attraction in town

Those "singing women" referred to as the "Saloon Singers" became the major attraction in the city.
In fact, they were the only game in town. Helen Morgan, Ruby Keeler and Texas Guinan became a legend. When the Prohibition came to an end in 1933, entrepreneurs began to open huge fancy nightclubs offering extravagant and lavish shows, and cabaret acts.
The legendary nightclubs like The Copacabana, The Cotillion, and The Diamond Horseshoe signed up Vaudeville celebrities like Sophie Tucker, Jimmy Durante and Frank Sinatra with various musical and dancing acts.
It was at that time in history that, famous cabaret singers were referred to as "Torch Singers."
Among the most famous ones were: Mabel Mercer, Bobby Short, Eartha Kitt, Pearl Bailey, Billie Holliday who performed at "The Vanguard," including Yul Brynner who worked at "The Blue Angel" as a Russian strolling guitarist. Yep! Believe it of not! One day, those nightclubs attractions will extend to New York's Greenwich Village.
Up on East 56th Street, the trendy Le Ruban Bleu showcased fabulous cabaret acts by Dorothy Loudon, Pat Carroll, Charlotte Rae, Carol Burnett and Kaye Ballard.

Helen Morgan, defined the term "Torch Singer."

Helen Morgan was and remains one of the first cabaret torch singers in America.

Born in Danville, Illinois, on August 2, 1900, Helen Riggins took the name Morgan in her childhood when her divorced mother remarried. Various conflicting accounts of her entry into show business survive, but she apparently obtained some voice training, sang in speakeasies, and in 1920 got a job in the chorus of Florenz Ziegfeld's Sally. More nightclub singing in Chicago and perhaps a beauty contest in Montreal led to a small role in George White's Scandals in 1925.

In that year she had an engagement at Billy Rose's Backstage Club, where the crowded conditions obliged her to perch on her accompanist's piano, an informal touch that soon became a trademark.

On Broadway, Morgan appeared in Americana (1926), Grand Guignol (1927), and Show Boat (1927), in which she was a sensation singing "Bill" and "Can't Help Lovin' Dat Man."

She starred in Sweet Adeline (1929), in which she sang "Don't Ever Leave Me" and "Why Was I Born?" Her later shows, less successful, include The Ziegfeld Follies of 1931, Memory (1934), George White's Scandals of 1936, and A Night at the Moulin Rouge (1939).

She also appeared in a number of motion pictures, including Applause (1929), Roadhouse Nights (1930), Sweet Music (1935), Frankie and Johnnie (1935), and Show Boat (1936).

Morgan's real strength, however, was as a club singer.

Her small, pale appearance and her sweet, artless, and blues-tinged voice made her the ideal performer of the new sort of popular song that was being written in the 1920s and '30s; ironic, sometimes bitter, distinctly urban, and full of the disappointment, loneliness, and joyless hedonism that filled the smoky clubs. Morgan died in Chicago, on October 8, 1941.

*** *** ***

Helen Morgan.

Ruby Keeler

Other famous nightclubs were The Purple Onion and The Bon Soir. Dame Sybil Bruncheon was one of the most visible patrons. One day at The Bon Soir in the early 1950's, Mike Nichols and Elaine May will begin their soaring careers, and in the early 1960's, it will showcase acts by future stars like Kaye Ballard and the young Barbra Streisand.

Dame Sybil Bruncheon.

224

May Irwin

Of Scottish ancestry, May Irwin was born Georgina May Campbell (not Ada Campbell, as many historians claim) in Whitby, Ontario, Canada. Her parents were Robert E. and Jane Draper Campbell. Her father died when she was young, and May turned to the theater to become self- supporting. With sister Adeline Flora Campbell (born on February 8, 1875, and known professionally as Flora or Flo Irwin), she went on stage, doing a singing specialty.

A.D. Storms stated in *The Players' Blue Book*, according to Jim Walsh in the July 1963 issue of *Hobbies*, that the Irwin Sisters made their debut at the Theatre Comique in Rochester, New York, on January 8, 1875; the book *Famous Actresses*, written by Lewis C. Strang (quoted by Walsh in the June 1963 issue of

Hobbies), stated that the debut was in Buffalo in December, and the girls opened with "Sweet Genevieve."

The Irwin Sisters appeared at Tony Pastor's Theatre on September 13, 1877, working there for the next six years.

When the act was dissolved, May Irwin worked solo. From 1883 to 1887 she was with Daly's company.

During that time she traveled twice to London to perform. May Irwin became a leading Vaudeville's performer of the 1890s. Best-known as a "coon- shouter," she introduced "The Bully" to stage audiences.

In his autobiography *After The Ball: Forty Years of Melody* (New York: Frank-Maurice, Inc, 1926), composer Charles K. Harris credits Irwin for popularizing "After the Ball" in New York City in early 1892.

Her "Crappy Dan" was popular enough in 1898 for Len Spencer to record it as a Columbia cylinder.

Columbia's 1898 catalog identified it as "May Irwin's hit." (From Tim Graycik's biography.)

Irwin's first starring role on the stage was in *The Widow Jones*, which opened on September 16, 1895, and featured the famous "Bully Song," or "The Bully."

The Famous Kiss:
A kissing scene from the hit show was filmed in 1896 by Edison's film company. Irwin was kissed by stage partner John Rice (father of singer Gladys Rice).

The film was not originally projected onto screens in theaters (the "Projecting Kinetoscope" came a little later) but was watched by individuals who purchased tickets at Kinetoscope Parlors and looked into a machine's peep-hole (some machines were coin-operated).

The film's showing time is less than a minute. Without citing credible evidence, film historians routinely report that early viewers were scandalized by the kiss. This is improbable. The film footage is innocuous by any standards, and the fact that it was released means that *Edison* film makers believed that this kiss violated no standards of the times.

The film captures a moment from an actual stage production, and since stage audiences were not scandalized, it is unlikely that viewers of the film were.

Fay Templeton.

Fay Templeton

Born in Little Rock, Arkansas, on December 25, 1865, Fay Templeton was the daughter of theatrical parents--principals in the touring John Templeton Opera Company--and grew up entirely in that milieu.

She was carried onstage in infancy and had her first speaking part at age five. By the early 1880s, Templeton was touring the country with her own light opera company. Her ascent to fame began with her appearance in *Evangeline* in New York City in

1885. She made her London debut the following year in *Monte Cristo Junior*.

In a succession of extravaganzas over the next decade, she became celebrated equally for her singing, her acting, and her dark, seductive beauty. She appeared with the team of Joe Weber and Lew Fields in their burlesque Hurly Burly (1898), in which her talents for comedy and parody were realized. She starred in Weber and Fields's Fiddle-dee-dee (1900), Hoity Toity (1901), and Twirly Whirly (1902), all of which also featured Lillian Russell.

Photo: G. M. Cohan.

In 1906, Templeton starred in George M. Cohan's "Forty-five Minutes from Broadway," in which she introduced "Mary's a Grand Old Name" and "So Long, Mary." For a quarter-century thereafter, Templeton lived in semi retirement with her husband in Pittsburgh, Pennsylvania, emerging to appear in such productions as Weber and Fields's Hokey Pokey in 1912 and several versions of H.M.S. Pinafore. She appeared in the film Broadway to Hollywood (1933), and late in 1933 returned to Broadway in Jerome Kern's Roberta. She died in San Francisco on October 3, 1939. (Data: Encyclopaedia Britannica).

***   ***   ***

Note on Vaudeville variety:

Vaudeville's star Julian Eltinge was the only female impersonator in the history of showbiz to have a Broadway theater named after him. (It is now the AMC Empire movie multiplex on 42nd Street). Vaudeville's most visible entertainers were: May Irwin, Julian Eltinge and Fay Templeton.

Julian Eltinge as a female on the left. And on the right as Mr. Eltinge.

Chapter 12
The Ziegfeld Follies

*** *** ***

The Ziegfeld Follies

Some of the most beautiful and famous Ziegfeld girls (singers and dancers) were:

- Marilyn Miller,
- Lillian Lorraine,
- Billie Burke,
- Anna Held,
- Josephine Baker,
- Claire Luce,
- Paulette Goddard,
- Sophie Tucker,

- Ruth Etting,
- Irene Dunn,
- Billie Dove,
- Lupe Velez,
- Dolly Sisters (Identical Hungarian twins Jenny and Rose),
- Nora Bayes,
- Marilyn Vega,
- Myrna Darby,
- Hazel Forbes,
- Dolores, born Kathleen Rose. A stunning tall English beauty who was a popular fashion model when Ziegfeld hired her as a torch singer and dancer for his 1917 *Follies*.
- Gilda Gray, born Marianne Michalski who was a ravishing Polish dancer.

The film "Gilda" of 1949 starring Rita Hayworth was based on her colorful and steamy life.

Photo: "The Follies of 1907", the making of a Broadway legend.

Ruth Etting

Ruth Etting was one of the most popular singing stars of the late 1920s and early 1930s. Florenz Ziegfeld, who glorified Ruth in the Follies, rated her as "the greatest singer of songs" that he had managed in a forty-year career.

On radio she established herself as America's pre-eminent popular singer, continually voted in listener polls as the top female singer on the air.

Even though, radio and the recording industry were still in their early developing years, Ruth Etting recorded over 200 songs by such composers as Irving Berlin, Johnny Green, Richard Rodgers and Lorenz Hart.

She was a regular performer on at least eight network radio programs. She appeared in six Broadway shows, made three major full-length movies and was the featured performer in 35 movie -short subjects- between 1928 and 1936.

*** *** ***

Anonyma

Hazel Forbes

Drucilla Strain

Marilyn Miller

Lillian Lorraine

Irene Dunn

Paulette Goddard

Anna Held

According to American musicals historian, John Henric, it is impossible to discuss Florenz Ziegfeld, Jr.'s development as a showman without considering Anna Held's contribution to his life and career. Ziegfeld got his taste in clothes, knowledge of stage presentation, and even the idea for his *Follies* from her.

She was one of the first celebrities to win transatlantic fame, and a leading musical stage role for more than two decades. It is no exaggeration to say that she was one of the most remarkable women of her time.

Although she later insisted that she was a native Parisian, Helene Anna Held was born in Warsaw, the daughter of a German Jewish glove maker and his French wife. Her "official" birthday was March 18, 1873, but some sources suggest she was born five to eight years sooner. When anti-Semitic pogroms swept Poland in 1881, the Held family fled to Paris.

There, her father's health faded, and teenager Anna had to support her family as a sweat shop seamstress. She occasionally sang in the streets to earn extra pennies. After her father died in 1884, Anna and her mother went to live with relatives in London. There, she was cast in several Yiddish musicals by the legendary actor-manager Jacob Adler. Held developed a unique stage presence over the next three years. She returned to Paris, where her rolling eyes, eighteen inch waist and naughty songs made Held a major star in the finest cafes. She increased her fame by such shrewd gestures as riding horses astride (rather than side-saddle), and by being one of the first women to ride those new inventions, the bicycle and motorcar.

She had an affair with wealthy South American gambler Maximo Carrera, and they married barely in time to legitimize the birth of their daughter Liane (sometime around 1895.) The child was raised in a convent, and the uncaring parents both went back to their separate lives. Anna's primary benefit from this marriage was that it gave her the excuse to convert to Catholicism. While she cared little for religion, she was anxious to escape the stigma faced by Jews in most of Europe. It also made it easier for her to perpetuate the myth that she was a native born French woman – a claim she clung to long after the press had proven otherwise.

Anna resumed her career, touring Germany and England with success.

She was appearing at London's Palace Music Hall in 1896 when the brash American producer Florenz Ziegfeld Jr. bribed his way into her dressing room. Ziegfeld wanted Held to appear in an upcoming Broadway production, and offered her the then-staggering sum of $1,500 a week. Anxious to get away from her husband's mounting gambling debts, Anna Held was quite willing to make the trip.

Thanks to Ziegfeld's masterful publicity (and his selective bribery of the press), Held's name and photo soon appeared in every newspaper and souvenir shop in New York.

By the time she arrived in the U.S., she was a ready-made celebrity. *A Parlor Match* (1896) was the story of a clever hobo who hoodwinks a gullible millionaire out of his valuables. At one point, the hobo uses a rigged "spirit cabinet," producing performing "ghosts" to prove that his victim's house is haunted. Anna Held appeared as one of these phony phantoms, singing her popular hit, "Won't You Come and Play With Me?"

> I wish you'd come and play with me,
> For I have such a way with me,
> A way with me, a way with me.
> I have such a nice little way with me,
> Do not think it wrong

*** *** ***

Anna Held
The talk of the town and the milk bath gossip

Her charming, suggestive delivery and outrageous French accent made a tremendous hit, and on stage, she had to sing several encores. After the show, a wild group of admirers (no doubt paid off by Ziegfeld) unhooked her carriage from its horses and pulled her through the streets.

Most critics were less than impressed by Held's performance, but she was the talk of New York. Whenever she was photographed, Held preferred poses that showcased her petite waist.

Always in search of a fresh publicity angle, Ziegfeld got an idea from the milky bath mixture Held used to condition her skin. He informed the press that Miss Anna Held bathed in several gallons of fresh milk every day, and reinforced the story by saying he had returned one shipment from a local dairy because it had gone sour.

Anna Held

The dairy owner sued Ziegfeld for libel and the hoax was eventually revealed – but Held's name made headlines every step of the way. At its time, the milk bath incident made titillating headlines for weeks and supposedly started a brief fad; an auspicious beginning for Ziegfeld's aggressive publicity blitz for Anna Held as a daring European performer. "The name of the young woman became as well known in this country as the name of the President," the New York World declared a year after her arrival. (Additional data: Linda Mizejewski, Ziegfeld Girl: Image and Icon in Culture and Cinema (Durham, NC: Duke University Press, 1999).

Over the next twelve years, Ziegfeld featured Anna Held in seven Broadway musicals tailored to showcase her charms. Each one ran in New York before going on tour (where most shows made their real profits at that time), but Held's first few shows were not the smash hits she and Ziegfeld had hoped for. In 1897, Held wrangled a divorce from Maximo Carerra. She and Ziegfeld had been living together for some years, but they now declared to friends that they were married.

They never went through the formality of a ceremony -- theirs was a "common law" union.

This spared Anna Held any wrangling with the Catholic Church, and made it easier for Ziegfeld to keep his options open for the future.

*** *** ***

Billie Burke

Billie Dove

Dorothy Knapp

Gilda Ray

Chapter 13
The Queens and Flashy Dashy Super Stars of the Early Era of American Entertainment

*** *** ***

Chapter 13
The Queens and Flashy Dashy Super Stars of the Early Era of American Entertainment

Josephine Baker

Josephine Baker was an internationally famous Afro-American entertainer. She began her career in the early 1920's as a chorus dancer in black musical comedies and in black nightclubs in New York City. She did not become a star until she moved to Paris in 1925, where she performed in black revues at the Folies Bergere and other Parisian music halls.

She also owned a nightclub.

Her rhythmic dancing and flamboyant stage presence made her a sensation by the late 1920's. Baker returned to the United States to perform in the Ziegfeld Follies of 1936. For a time, she operated a nightclub in New York City. She retired in 1956 to devote more time to her family of 12 adopted children. She raised her family on her estate in France until financial difficulties forced the sale of the property.

Baker often returned to the stage in the 1960's and early 1970's. She was born on June 3, 1906, in St. Louis, Missouri. She died on April 12, 1975.

*** *** ***

Josephine Baker

Claire Luce

After marrying her second husband, publisher Henry R. Luce, Claire Luce (1903-1987) wrote three successful plays: The Women (1936), Kiss the Boys Goodbye (1938) and Margin for Error (1939).

She later served as a war correspondent before representing Connecticut in Congress from 1943-1947. She was keynote speaker at the 1944 Republican National Convention.

In 1953, Claire Luce became the first American woman ambassador to a major country when President Dwight Eisenhower appointed her ambassador to Italy (1953-1956).

In 1983, four years before her death, Claire Luce received the Presidential Medal of Freedom.

Rodgers who was one of London's leading theatre photographers from the 1930s until his death in 1970, took many photos of Luce. Also, he was the sole photographer of both ballet and opera at the Royal Opera House during the 1950s.

*** *** ***

The Legendary Stars: Or, used to be!!

From left to right: Ruth Etting, Lupe Velez, Gilda Ray.

From left to right: Sophie Tucker, Marylin Miller.

From left to right: Irene Dunn, Paulette Goddard, Billie Dove.

The first American musicals and cabaret acts.

Photo: Niblo's Garden, a 3,200 seat theatre at the corner of Broadway and Prince Streets.

The early American musicals were performed as British ballad comic operas. The very first musical was "Flora". It was performed in 1735 in Charleston and moved to New York in 1750. The first national musical "The Archers" written by Benjamin Carr and William Dunlap premiered on April 18, 1796 at the John Street Theater in New York City.

263

In 1800, the musical melodrama genre came to life. The first blockbuster was "The Black Crook" a 240 performer extravagant musical play which premiered at the fabulous Niblo Garden. "The Black Crook" was condemned by ethicists and moralists as a flesh show, and libeled as an immoral production.
The producers profited from this negative publicity.
Consequently, the show sold tickets like hot cakes. It became an instant success. This brought fortune to William Wheatley and his associates. The musical play was played and replayed for several years and was richly revived on Broadway.
The troupe's prima ballerina, Marie Bonfanti, became an international celebrity and the toast of the city of New York. Some historians tend to believe that this famous and infamous production paved the way for burlesques.

But first came Vaudeville and burlesque!

First came Vaudeville and burlesque followed, leading toward a new Broadway musicals genre.
The style of the era was represented by favorites such as the Showboat' "Ol' Man River" which was first played by the Paul Whiteman Orchestra in January 11, 1928 and the various tunes of Gershwin's songs and ballads, particularly those of "Porgy and Bess" which were first performed by Rudy Vallee at the Alvin Theater in New York in 1935.
At the same time, Vaudeville remained strong and prospered thanks to the first ladies of Vaudeville:

- Ethel Waters,
- Baby Peggy,
- Nora Bayes,
- Maggie Cline,
- May Irwin,

- Ida Cox,
- Marie Dressler,
- Judy Garland,
- Gilda Gray,
- Alberta Hunter,

- Texas Guinan,

- Clarice Vance,
- Trixie Friganza,
- Fifi D'Orsay,
- Marilyn Miller,

- Florence Mills,
- Helen Morgan,
- Mae Questel,
- Ma Reiney,
- Lillian Russell,
- Alberta Hunter,

- Sophie Tucker,

- Patsy Kelly,
- Cissie Loftus,

- Mary Irwin,
- Sissieretta Jones

In the fifties, the cabaret surfaced in the United States; a "typically American style" founded on American standards and works by American composers music and pioneers.

It was a safe, polite, entertaining and delightful American art and entertainment platform.

Famous and less known artists performed quite frequently on stage, across the country, but New York remained the world stage.

Maggie Cline

Ethel Waters

Ida Cox

Alberta Hunter

Chapter 14
The golden years of live entertainment on radio.

*** *** ***

Chapter 14
The golden years of live entertainment on radio.

THE EARLY SOLO VOCALISTS

"He's a great singer, but ya know, you can't make it without a band. Every singer has got to have a band behind him." - Bandleader Tommy Dorsey, February 1942.

In January 1942, the 26 year old Frank Sinatra took the world of entertainment by storm. Thousands of young girls fell in love with him, and hundreds fainted every time he performed on stage. Female bobby-soxers screamed and screamed and rushed to touch his face amid hysteria and bursting passion.

For long time, he has been performing as a solo singer with the Tommy Dorsey and his Orchestra, but now Sinatra realized that his ready for a solo career, alone and on his own, even if his boss Tommy Dorsey believed Sinatra was "a damn fool" for considering it.

Dorsey was convinced that Sinatra will never make it without his band. He was wrong! The idea that a band vocalist would go out on his or her own, without the promotional support of a popular orchestra, was absurd and unrealistic in the 1940s. Many singers of the era preferred to stick to their bands for financial security purposes. Sinatra was different.

He had the support and loyalty of thousands and thousands of teenagers and young adults. At that time in history, radio sponsors began to recognize the vast economic buying power of young audiences and teenagers.

But one question haunted their minds: How much money those teenagers could spend or how much goods and merchandise would they buy? Sinatra was not concerned at all, because he was the first and ultimate superstar of the postwar years. Sinatra's decision ushered in, a new daring trend in showbiz. And he did it at a time when the popularity of big bands began to decline for many reasons.

The United States was in war. Consequently, wartime restrictions on steel, rubber, tires and fuel made it so difficult for big band to tour regularly and appear on radio programs across the country. Besides, big bands could no longer record their music as often as they wished, because shellac and other products used in manufacturing the 78RPM records were in short supply. Indeed, this short supply in materials decreased the production and sales of records. But this would not affect the career of a solo vocalist touring the country without a big band.

Photo: James Petrillo, the powerful president of the AFM.

Add to the fact, that between 1941 and 1945, many big bands members were drafted.

And to make things worst, in August 1942, a recording ban was imposed by the American Federation of Musicians, generated by a bitter dispute concerning copyrights, royalties and compensations for musicians and composers works and their recordings.

The ban lasted until 1943 and the case would not be resolved until 1944. Many non-union singers benefited from this crisis, because they were not forbidden to record their own songs. Of course, solo singers had to pay for recording their songs, studio time, and above all, they had to find professional musicians. But this was a minor concern, because they found out that they could record their songs with salaried studio musicians. And instead of using big bands and/or a large number of professional musicians, daring solo vocalists used small but effective choral accompaniment, and in many instances, they substituted with their own vocals dubbed over several tracks recorded in Mexico City.

Not to forget the fact that record companies were fully aware that working with solo star singers was much much cheaper than working with a large band and a pompous famous bandleader.

So record companies decided to replace big bands with studio musicians and small combos to accompany solo vocalists.

Record producers also realized that it is far cheaper to work with a small band composed from studio musicians, because they did not have to pay lots of money for an arranger to write orchestration and arrangements for a large number of musicians and musical instruments, as it was the case with big bands.

Sinatra welcomed the idea. This allowed him to choose his own arrangers. Sharp and shrewd, Sinatra was able to convince the legendary Axel Stordahl, the musical arranger of Dorsey to quit Dorsey's band and work for him.

Sinatra opened the door for many non-union arrangers, and work was abundant. Later on, many stars of the era will imitate Sinatra and hire their own arrangers.

The legendary Axel Stordahl. Now, of course, forgotten!!

Early Stars of the Music Business:

By the end of the war, singers like Frank Sinatra, Perry Como, Helen Forrest, Dick Haymes, Jo Stafford, Andy Russell, were the superstars of the music business.

Photos from L to R:
1-Dick Haymes was born on September 13, 1916 in Buenos Aires, Argentina. He died from lung cancer on March 28, 1980 in Los Angeles, California. He renounced his United States citizenship in 1944 and registered himself as resident alien. He starred in "Won Ton Ton", "The Dog Who Saved Hollywood" (26-May-1976), "One Touch of Venus" (Aug-1948), "The Shocking Miss Pilgrim" (4-Jan-1947), "State Fair" (29-Aug-1945), "Irish Eyes Are Smiling" (19-Oct-1944).

2-Jo Stafford was born on November 12, 1917 in Coalinga, California. In the early 1990s, Stafford won a huge breach-of-contract lawsuit against her former record label, which won her rights to all of her old recordings. Soon after, Stafford reactivated her Corinthian Record label. In 1966, she retired from the music business. But briefly, in 1977, she did the Jonathan and Darlene Edwards version of "Stayin' Alive." In 1990, Stafford sang at a ceremony honoring Frank Sinatra. Unquestionably, Stafford was one of the most popular singers of the post-war period.

Photos from L to R:

Helen Forrest was born on April 12, 1917 in Atlantic City, New Jersey. She died on Jul 11, 1999 in Los Angeles, California. Forrest was one of the more popular big band era singers. In her early career, she used many names, such as Bonnie Blue and The Blue Lady. In 1939, Shaw orchestra was disbanded, so Forrest joined Benny Goodman and sang with his band until 1941. It should be noted that in 1940, she recorded with Lionel Hampton and Nat King Cole's trio. In the early '60s, Forrest sang with Tommy Dorsey's Orchestra led by Sam Donahue. In 1994, arthritis forced her to retire. In 1999, Helen Forrest passed away from heart failure.

Perry Como was born on May 18, 1912 in Canonsburg, Pennsylvania. He died on May 12, 2001 in Jupiter, Florida. He was one of the most popular singers between the end of World War II and the rise of rock & roll in the mid-'50s. Before reaching stardom, Como worked as a singing barber in his hometown and toured with local bandleader Freddie Carlone. He got his big break in 1933 when he joined Ted Weems & His Orchestra. After the orchestra went out of business in 1942, Como hosted the "Supper Club", a successful CBS radio show, and this opened the door for him to sign a contract with RCA Victor Records in 1943. The 1945 film "A Song to Remember" put Como on the map. It was his big break. His biggest hit was "Till the End of Time". This song stayed ten weeks at the very top of the charts and became the biggest hit of the season. His 1948 NBC radio show earned him four Emmy Awards.

Jo Stafford

Helen Forrest

Andy Russell, Raul Reyes, Eva Reyes and The Copa Girls from the 1947
film "Copacabana".

Andy Russell.

The legendary Carmen Miranda.

"Copacabana" was Groucho Marx's first film without his brothers. Carmen Miranda played her familiar bubbly Brazilian role and doubled as a French chanteuse.

The film included the international hit "Tico, Tico" written by Sam Coslow. The cast consisted of Groucho Marx (Lionel Devereaux), Carmen Miranda (Carmen Novarro) Steve Cochran (Steve Hunt), Abel Green who played himself, Andy Russell who played himself, Gloria Jean (Anne), De Castro Sisters who played themselves, the fabulous dancers Raul Reyes and Eva Reyes, and The Copa Girls.

*** *** ***

Carmen Miranda, still remembered. But by whom?

Carmen Miranda

With the recording ban lifted, local radio stations geared toward disk jockey...it was the end of the big band era...

With the recording ban lifted, local radio stations geared toward disk jockey programs. By 1946, the golden era of the big bands came to an end and popular singers took over.

The era of solo singers just began; "Fibber McGee and Molly" featured Martha Tilton for 15 months; the King's Men vocal group lasted for 11 years.

Jack Benny began introducing an avalanche of solo singers and performers.

Martha Tilton

Martha Tilton.

Martha Tilton was born on November 14, 1915 in Corpus Christi, Texas. She died on December 8 2006 in Brentwood, California. She was one of the first artists to record for Capitol Records. In 1939, she had a hit with "And the Angels Sing" recorded with Benny Goodman.

Among her biggest hits were "I'll Walk Alone", a wartime song which got the 4th spot on the 1944 charts, "A Stranger in Town", and "I Should Care" both got the 10th place on the 1945 chart;

280

three other songs also topped the chart in 1947: "I Wonder, I Wonder, I Wonder", "How Are Things in Glocca Morra", and "That's My Desire."

In 1957, she recorded a very successful album "We Sing the Old Songs" with Curt Massey. Around 1959, both Tilton and Massey co-hosted a daily half-hour TV show in Los Angeles. The show lasted seven years.

Tilton voice was used several times in many motion pictures, and dubbed over other actresses' voices, to name a few:

Anne Gwynne, Barbara Stanwyck, and Martha O'Driscoll.

*** *** ***

Martha Tilton

Memorable shows, moments and live entertainment of the era.

The Best of Old Time Radio

From left to right: Lum Edwards and Abner Peabody. Willard Waterman.

Somewhere during that time in history...1930s, 1940s, and 1950s

The Andrews Sisters and The Firehouse Five Plus Two joined Bing Crosby's popular post-war series for Chesterfield Cigarettes on Wednesday, March 29, 1950.

Bing Crosby sang "You're Wonderful," and "Candy and Cake," and joined the Andrews Sisters in a delightful number titled "Lock, Stock and Barrel," and the Firehouse Five in a swinging Dixieland rendition of "Everybody Loves My Baby," and the girls performed a truly marvelous vocal version of the jazz standard "That's a Plenty."

Al Jolson, "The World's Greatest Entertainer" stared in a broadcast from his legendary 1940s series for Kraft Foods, which also featured pianist/comedian Oscar Levant. In one of the best shows, first heard on Thursday, October 21, 1948, Jolson took center stage to reenact his glory days at the Wintergarden Theater and performed a variety of timeless numbers, including such gems as "For Me and My Gal," "More Than You Know," "About a Quarter to Nine," "Toot Toot Tootsie," "You Made Me Love You," and "Without a Song." Chester Lauck and Norris Goff became the new owners of Arkansas own Jot Em Down Stor, and delivered a rare broadcast from the long-running and beloved comedy serial that put Pine Ridge on the map. In a program first heard on Wednesday, April 12, 1944 and sponsored by Alka Seltzer, an all-knowing Lum Edwards delivered a spirited lecture on the evils of wealth to a dubious and doubtful Abner Peabody. Willard Waterman stared in a title role in a broadcast from a The Great Gildersleeve, a much-loved family situation comedy.

In that program, first heard on Wednesday, November 5, 1952, Gildy has been invited by the mayor to play a round of golf. After taking a few practice swings, complete with "constructive" criticism from his nephew Leroy (Walter Tetley), he got a crick in his neck and took a trip to his doctor's office. Dinah Shore stared with announcer Harry Von Zell in a musical comedy series from the mid-1940s.

From left to right: Dinah Shore with Harry Von Zell. Dick Powell.

In that episode, first broadcast on Thursday, May 3, 1945, Dinah shared the microphone with guests Jim and Marion Jordan who, as Fibber McGee and Molly, invited the performer to 79 Wistful Vista to present her with a trophy as the outstanding singer of 1945.

Radio's longest running family drama, "One Man's Family," created by the legendary Carlton E. Morse is steaming. In that program, originally heard on Tuesday, December 23, 1952, the Barbour's son Paul arrived home just in time for the family's traditional Christmas celebration..."The Cinnamon Bear", a memorable radio classic, has entertained children of all ages for more than seventy years. In the first episode of that timeless series, first broadcast Friday, November 26, 1937, Judy and Jimmy found Paddy O'Cinnamon hiding among the Christmas decorations in their attic.

From left to right: Jack Maher. Les Brown with Doris Day.

They learned that the Crazy Quilt Dragon has stolen a gleaming silver star, intended for the top of their Christmas tree, and the Cinnamon Bear invited them to go after him. Complete with that familiar pipe organ theme music, Orphan Annie in a 1937 episode -complete with Ovaltine commercials voiced by Pierre Andre, heard the story about the Wright Brothers' historic first flight at Kitty Hawk.

Lew Ayers and Lionel Barrymore stared in the first program of The Story of Dr. Kildare, a syndicated radio series, based on the popular and long-running MGM movies and first broadcast on February 1, 1950. A young woman named Angela Kester is a promising young concert pianist, but she is afflicted with obsessive/compulsive disorder and extreme paranoia.

After she attempts suicide, Dr. Kildare must consider a risky operation to save her from sinking into insanity.
In Crime Classics, Elliot Lewis' cult radio series offered a memorable and entertaining episode, first heard over CBS on Wednesday, November 11, 1953. In "Blackbeard's Fourteenth Wife: Why She Was No Good For Him," William Conrad portrayed Edward Teach - better known as Blackbeard the Pirate - who arrived in Nassau in 1714 and married a sixteen-year-old girl who drove him to his greatest fame...and ultimately to his doom...Les Brown and his Band of Renown broadcast from Woodrow Wilson General Hospital in Virginia, a swinging wartime program featured vocals by Doris Day, Gordon Drake and Butch Stone.
First heard over the Blue Network on Thursday, May 25, 1944.

285

This fifteen-minute program was later rebroadcast by the Armed Forces Radio Service.

Dick Powell stared as the first "Singing Detective" in an engrossing program from Richard Diamond, Private Detective, a light hearted action/adventure series, originally broadcast on Sunday, February 19, 1950.

In this entry, the detective is asked by his old friend Lieutenant Levinson to look into a case involving stolen jewels, a murdered husband, and a beautiful widow who doesn't seem particularly sorry to have found her husband dead. O. Henry's "Robin Hood of the Old West" is riding again in a 1953 episode from The Cisco Kid, a popular syndicated series, starring Jack Mather as Cisco and Harry Lang as his sidekick, Pancho.

In that program, the Sundance Gang, led by the ruthless and notorious Sundance Kid, is using a cave outside Cimarron, New Mexico as a hideout.

One Sunday morning, they ride in to loot the town -- but Sundance is soon talked out of it by a beautiful and fearless newcomer named Milo Normandy.

*** *** ***

"The Big Show": A huge musical production.

Many consider "The Big Show" to be the most important one of Meredith Wilson's radio career. This high-budget show had everything – a 44 piece orchestra, a 16 voice chorus, talented and experienced writers, top stars as guests, and fascinating dramatic performances. Meredith Willson was the program's presiding maestro, and was ably assisted by the great Tallulah Bankhead. His "chiffon swing" musical arrangements and his excellent comedic timing elevated the show to truly high standards. During his association with the AFRS he met George Burns and Gracie Allen, who were doing, at the time, their Thursday night comedy program, "Maxwell House Coffee Time."

They invited him to create "chiffon" musical arrangements for their show in 1945. But that was not all; he was also asked to act with them, something he did extremely well, taking up the role of a shy bandleader, dying to get married but terribly afraid of women. His performance fitted perfectly with the zany antics of Gracie Allen through the three years he spent on the show.

Then, in 1948, he created his own show, a variety series called "The Meredith Willson Show." In this show he created "The Talking People," a vocal quintet featuring Betty Allen, Bob Hanlon, John Rarig, Maxwell Smith, and Norma Zimmer.

They created an intriguing way of reciting the show's Jell-O commercials together, creating what was felt to be a shimmering effects, emulating the shimmy of the dessert.

On "The Big Show," Willson often referred to his home town, Mason City, Iowa, in a humorous and interesting way. But he had other ideas as well for his childhood experiences, and for eight years and many revisions, he tried to create a tribute to his home state by writing a musical about it. In 1957, the musical appeared on Broadway; "The Music Man" became an instant hit and a landmark stage musical. The songs, written by Willson, became classics. These include "76 Trombones", "Til There Was You", "Music Man", "'Til I met You", "May the Good Lord Bless and Keep You" and "It's Beginning to Look a Lot Like Christmas." The success of "The Music Man" convinced Willson to continue creating musical theatre, and his other shows include such memorable musicals as The "Unsinkable Molly Brown," "Here's Love" and a musical version of the film "Miracle on 34th Street."

Screen and stage legend, **Tallulah Bankhead** in "Faithles." She was born on
January 31, 1902 in Huntsville, Alabama. She died from pneumonia and
influenza on December 12, 1968 in New York.
Bankhead's contributions to "THE BIG SHOW" were enormous.

But despite his success on Broadway, he did not leave radio, and after the ending of "The Big Show" he created a variety program called "Encore" which often featured Marguerite Piazza and Robert Merril (who was also a frequent visitor on "The Big Show"). Interested in early TV, he became a panelist on the quiz show "The Name's the Same," produced by the prolific Mark Goodson and Bill Todman team.

George Burns and wife Gracie Allen.

Avalanches of unforgettable stars and legends...

Tallulah brought to her show both high and low brow guests, including Beatrice Lillie, Dennis King (who is featured in a dramatic adaptation of Herman Melville's "Billy Budd"), Jack Carson and Ed Wynn.

Ed interpreted Lauritz Melchior's operatic performance (this time it's "Tannhauser"...but it still sounds like "Carmen"). Later in the program, Carson and Fred Allen did the same for Tallulah's rendition of "I'll Be Seeing You." Bing Crosby and Bob Hope were heard on the Chesterfield commercial.

The performers were Ed Wynn, Jack Carson, Beatrice Lillie ("Not Wanted on the Voyage"), Dennis King, Lauritz Melchior (Wagner's "Dreams"), Fred Allen, Portland Hoffa,

The West Point Choir ("The Corps"), announcer Ben Grauer, Meredith Willson and his Orchestra and Chorus and Tallulah Bankhead. Aired on Sunday, February 18, 1951 on NBC. It was sponsored by Anacin, Chesterfield and RCA Victor.

From L to R: Judy Holliday. Monty Woolley.

From L to R: Uta Hagen. Jack Haley played the Tin Man in The Wizard of Oz).

From L to R: Paul Kelly. 3-Ethel Merman spared verbally with Tallulah Bankhead. Three of them shared the spotlight in "THE BIG SHOW".

Photo: Jack Haley playing the Tin Man in The Wizard of Oz.

Judy Holliday returned to the program...and she's still needling Tallulah about her love life. Talloo also crossed verbal swords with Monty Woolley and then accompanied him in re-creating his most famous stage/movie role in a scene from the Moss Hart-George S. Kaufman play "The Man Who Came to Dinner." Later in the program, Judy, Jack Haley, and Olsen and Johnson sent up the same scene. Uta Hagen and Paul Kelly also performed scenes from Clifford Odetts' "The Country Girl." Bing Crosby and Bob Hope were heard on the Chesterfield commercial.

291

The performers were Jack Haley warbled a hilarious tune about all the Irish talent in Hollywood (Haley played the Tin Man in The Wizard of Oz), Uta Hagen, Monty Woolley, Judy Holliday, Ole Olsen and Chic Johnson, Paul Kelly, Robert Merrill (Verdi's "Di Provenza"), announcer Ed Herlihy, Meredith Willson and his Orchestra and Chorus ("Military Polka") and Tallulah Bankhead. The 18th episode of the show was a tribute to the great Irving Berlin -- but before the show-stopping finale, Ethel Merman spared verbally with Talloo, Portland Hoffa sang "Sweet Marie" (with hubby Fred Allen accompanying her on the banjo), and Herb Shriner did one of his classic "Hoosier" routines. Clive Brook, Hugh Riley and Margaret Phillips performed an excerpt from Philip Barry's "Second Threshold," adapted by Robert Sherwood. Bing Crosby and Bob Hope were as usual heard on the Chesterfield commercial.

The performers were Clive Brook, Ethel Merman, Frankie Laine ("Swamp Girl"), Fred Allen, Herb Shriner, Hugh Riley, Margaret Philips, Margaret Truman ("Love is Where You Find It"), Portland Hoffa, announcer Ed Herlihy, Meredith Willson and his Orchestra and Chorus ("Aba Dabba Honeymoon") and Tallulah Bankhead, of course! This episode was aired on Sunday, March 4, 1951(NBC.) The 19th episode featured a compendium of comedy veterans: Bob Burns, "The Arkansas Traveler", told stories from his hometown of Van Buren, Arkansas -- and played the bazooka to boot; Smith and Dale performed their immortal "Dr. Kronkheit" routine with Jean Courtney as the nurse; and tall tales emanated from Baron Munchausen (Jack Pearl) to the amazement of straight man Cliff Hall ("Vas you dere, Sharlie?"). Jimmy Durante was reunited with Vaudeville partner Eddie Jackson (the two men sang "Bill Bailey") and Celeste Helm and Talloo dished the dirt about each other.

The performers were Billy Eckstine ("If"), Bob Burns, Celeste Holm ("The Happy Ending"), Jimmy Durante, Eddie Jackson, Evelyn Knight ("I Remember the Cornfields"), Jack Pearl, Cliff Hall, Jean Courtney, Joe Smith and Charlie Dale, announcer Ed Herlihy, Meredith Willson and his Orchestra and Chorus ("Thoughts While Strolling") and Tallulah Bankhead as usual! The episode was aired on Sunday, March 11, 1951.

Jerome Cowan, Vera Zorina, and Phil Baker in a scene from the 1938 film
"The Goldwyn Follies," with music by George Gershwin.
Phil Baker reproduced a similar scenario for Tallulah.

For the 20th episode, Ethel Waters recreated her celebrated stage role as Hagar in a dramatized scene from "Mamba's Daughters" and Fred Allen told the sad tale of how a family was ripped apart by the quiz show phenomenon...just before Talloo auditioned to appear on Phil Baker's radio show.

Bing Crosby and Bob Hope were waiting to be paid before they do their commercials for Chesterfield. The performers are Phil Baker (who played "Stardust" on his accordion), Johnny Burke, Eddie Cantor ("Oh! Oh! Oh! There's Nothing Like Radio"), Eddie Fisher ("Bring Back the Thrill"), Ella Fitzgerald ("Sometimes I'm Happy"), Fred Allen, Portland Hoffa, Jan Peerce ("May the Good Lord Bless and Keep You"), Ethel Waters ("Happiness is Just a Thing Called Joe"), Martin Blaine, announcer Ed Herlihy, Meredith Willson and his Orchestra and Chorus ("Here Comes the Springtime") and Tallulah Bankhead. The episode aired on Sunday, March 18, 1951.

*** *** ***

293

Ethel Merman and Eddie Cantor.

"The Big Show" had serious competition.

First, the rival Columbia Broadcasting System featured Jack Benny, Edgar Bergen & Charlie McCarthy, and Amos 'n' Andy (Freeman Gosden and Charles Correll). Second, television was beginning to attract audiences away from radio.

But that was where Tallulah Bankhead came in.

She was a huge star, with such stage hits as "Private Lives" and "The Skin of Our Teeth" fresh in the audiences' memory, and extensive radio experience, since she had already appeared with Bergen & McCarthy, Eddie Cantor, and Fred Allen, and performed in the dramatic "The Radio Reader's Digest" and "The Screen Director's Playhouse."

But most important, she also had glamour, unpredictability, tremendous comedic talent, and a huge ego that amused the audience.

The talented writers cashed on her merits creating a sharp, venomous exchange between her and the guests and often featuring the well-known feud she had with Bette Davis.

Selma Diamond

The writing team was legendary. The chief writer was Goodman Ace ("Easy Aces" with his wife Jane), and his team included George Foster, Morton Green, Frank Wilson, Selma Diamond, and Fred Alan (who was not credited). With producer-director Dee Engelbach's special touch, and Meredith Willson's "chiffon" arrangements, the show was bound to succeed.

Willson and Tallulah Bankhead worked together perfectly, and they got huge laughs when he would play her stooge, salaaming her and addressing her with "Thank you, Miss Bankhead, Sir." Unfortunately, the show did not last.
It was intelligently scheduled by NBC at 6:30 P.M. on Sundays, but the audiences would not give up "The Jack Benny Show" that appeared on CBS at 7:00 P.M. and the Ed Sullivan's "Toast of the Town" on television. So in spite of huge publicity campaigns, including taking the show to Paris and London, the show lost nearly one million dollars, and was canceled on April 20, 1952.

*** *** ***

Celebrities of the era who were expert in handling the microphone

Lowell Thomas, circa 1930.

Eugene Harold "Buddy" Weed, taken in 1947 for Downbeat Magazine.
Buddy Weed (1918-1997)—Buddy Weed's piano style was extra-
ordinarily refined.

Durward Kirby

Sir Harry Lauder, 1870-1950, "Laird of the music hall."

Herbert Marshall

Rex Dale
WCKY program host Rex Dale interviews Ms. Gloria Swanson.

Chapter 15
Broadway's Vanished Era

Chapter 15
Broadway's Vanished Era

Oscar Hammerstein in front of his theater at Times Square, New York, 1900

Tony Pastor

Tony Pastor had managed Variety Theater since its very first opening in New York City in 1865. At that time in history, there was a "Ladies mile" of fancy department stores in the upper teens on 5th and 6th Avenue.

Gossip has it that "from 14th Street down, the men were earning it, and from 14th Street up, the women were spending it." Pastor recognized that he could attract an afternoon audience of the women who were shopping at those department stores.

So he conveniently billed his theater as "refined vaudeville", and it worked like a charm. In no time, Vaudeville joints followed his example.

***   ***   ***

The Cohans at curtain call (from L to R: George, Josephine, Jerry "father" and mother).

Vaudeville legendary vocalist Anna Wheaton.

Photo: "Rehearsal - Ned Wayburn's Town Topics, New York City 1915."

Photos from L to R: 1-Ned Wayburn with Alma Gluck. 2-Ned Wayburn.

Ned Wayburn (1874-1942) was a big name in showbiz, and particularly in dance.

He developed tab shows for children. Wayburn staged the very first debut act for Fred Astaire and Adele Astaire, who were his students.

Many of his acts were seen on the Orpheum circuit of West Coast and Mid-West theaters, and included the various Dainty June acts that toured on the Orpheum circuit before Dainty June became June Havoc and Rose Louise became Gypsy Rose Lee.

Evelyne Law.

Between 1910 and 1930, Wayburn taught many famous people and mega stars how to dance, such as:

- Ann Pennington,
- Eddie Cantor,
- Gilda Gray,
- Marilyn Miller,
- Ada Mae Weeks,
- Evelyne Law,
- The Marx Brothers
- The Ziegfield's Girls.

Ned Wayburn was one of Broadway's first dance-conscious directors and choreographers. He directed 10 shows and six of Ziegfeld's Follies.

Adele Astaire

Photos from L to R: 1-Fred Astaire and Adele Astaire. 2- Young Freddie (Fred Aster) and Delly (Adele Astaire).

The Astaires began training early.
Their mother, Ann Austerlitz wasn't happy to stay in Omaha, Nebraska. When her husband Frederick lost his position as a salesman for a brewery victim of Prohibition, she thought that it was time to see if her two children (Fred and Adele) could make it in Vaudeville.

So, Mrs. Austerlitz and her two children took the train to New York City. Upon her arrival to Manhattan, she decided that the children should be called "Astaire." Soon enough, Fred and Adele were placed in a skit based on *Cyrano de Bergerac*. Being much taller than Fred, Adele played Cyrano, and Fred, in a long silly blond wig, became Roxane!

*** *** ***

Helen Dauvray

In 1884, in New York, Helen Dauvray became a huge star. She married *New York Giant's* Johnnie Ward, the most elegant, and talkative baseball player of the era, later on to regret it, for she went through one of the most horrible divorces of all time. She made a fortune playing on Broadway. Her most memorable role is the lead she took in 1885 Bronson Howard's hit "One of Our Girls." After divorcing Monsieur Playboy Johnnie Ward, she married Albert Winterhalter, a military officer stationed in San Francisco, and officially announced her retirement in 1896.

A few years later, hubby Winterhalter became admiral, and Helen Dauvray joined the high society, enjoying a comfortable life until her death in 1926.

Former husband Ward tried to reconcile with her, but she warned him to stop all his "maneuvers", otherwise she will put him on a boat and ship him to the other end of the globe guarded by two of her husband's lieutenants.

*** *** ***

Katherine Alexander
(1898-1981)

In 1924's, Alexander was a huge name on Broadway.
She is remembered for her performance in the 1917 "The Awful Mrs. Eaton."
Soon after, she married William Brady, the producer of the show. She excelled in playing the role of a passionate young woman. She made it big, very big in a series of musicals, such as: "The Queen's Husband" (1928), "Hotel Universe" (1930), and "The Left Bank" (1931). She appeared as Anna Sutter in the worst box office disaster of the 1930s "Sutter's Gold", but with the support

of MGM studio she survived to become one of Bette Davis best supporting actresses, and she shined in several movies such as "That Certain Woman" and "Now, Voyager."

*** *** ***

Dorothy Dickson

Dorothy Dickson (1893-1995) began her career as a dancer in summer of 1914 in the public dance hall, "Jardin de Dance", in New York. By April 1917, she was billed as "The Greatest Dance Personality in the World.", and this propaganda claim attracted Ziegfeld and he hired her on the spot in his 1917 Follies. In 1918, she teamed up with her husband Charles Hyson in Jerome Kern's "Rock-a-bye Baby."
 Her success was so great that the New York Times on May 26, 1918, published an extensive article declaring her the successor of Irene Castle and the queen of ballroom dancing. During WWI, she entertained the troops on stage, free of charge.
In 1919 she appeared in the operetta "Lassie", and George M. Cohan's "The Royal Vagabond." In 1920, she starred in 3 films and took the lead in Ziegfeld's "Sally" in London.
Her magnificent performance in "The Cabaret Girl" earned her the friendship of the Queen Mother, and established her as an international star. She lived to be 102, and was regarded as one of the greatest stage actresses in Great Britain.

*** *** ***

Ruth Chatterton

Ruth Chatterton (1893-1961). She was discovered at age 16 while visiting a friend in a stage stock company in New York. The manager spotted her and asked her to audition for a part. She did and she got the part. She became an overnight sensation when she performed in the premiere of the 1912 "The Rainbow." She had a broad vocal range.
"Daddy Long Legs" made her a Broadway star. In 1924, she appeared in "Madame X." In 1946, she produced, directed, and starred in "The Second Best Bed." She was a strong supporter of the newly formed state of Israel.

313

Ruth Chatterton turned to science fiction writing without relinquishing her stage and cinema career.

*** *** ***

Louise Dresser.

Louise Dresser

Louise Dresser (1887-1965).
She graced the stage and Broadway's musicals with her haute couture, savoire faire and panache. A Vaudeville singer and silent movie actress, Dresser was discovered and encouraged by songwriter Paul Dresser, who introduced her to his friends and showbiz producers as his sister. Legend has it that Paul Dresser gave her his name to boost her career. In 1906, Jack Norworth, composer of "Shine on Harvest Moon," became her first husband. Norworth took her to New York and convinced Lew Fields to use her as a vocalist in "About Town."
She wowed the audience and became a Broadway sensation. Her marriage to Nortworth lasted only three years. Paul Dresser got rid of Northworth and replaced him with Jack Gardner.
In those days, artists were commodity and products! For 12 years, she worked with the most powerful producers in New York. She is remembered for her roles in "The Matinee Idol", "The Candy Shop" and especially for playing Catherine the Great in Valentino's "The Eagle", and Marie de Nardi in "The Goose Woman." In 1929 she was nominated for the best actress academy award for "A Ship Comes In."

Photo: **Anne Pennington** was a huge name. From L to R: **Winnie Lightner, Ann Pennington, Nancy Welford** and **Lilyan Tashman** in the 1930 "Gold Diggers of Broadway."

Billie Dove (1902-1997)

Flo Ziegfeld saw the statuesque model on the cover of a magazine, and became interested in her. When he contacted her, he found out that she was only fourteen. He waited until she was 16 and hired in his 1919 Follies.

In 1920, she appeared in the "Midnight Frolic". Soon after, Ziegfeld began an affair with Billie Dove. His other Billie in real life, his wife, Billie Burke, knew about the affair, and behind his back, shipped Dove to Hollywood.

In 1923, Dove reached stardom on the silent screen.

*** *** ***

Billie Burke (1885-1970)

Billie Burke, the child of an heiress and a singing clown was the second wife of Florenz Ziegfeld. She was beautiful, wealthy and highly educated.

Burke was known for her tempestuous character, fine manners and graceful acting on stage. She began her career as a teenager singer in 1903, and became a sensation overnight. On New Year's Eve 1913, she met Florenz Ziegfeld at a ball and fell in love with him, to the chagrin of everybody.

Friends advised her to forget about Ziegfeld, for he was known for his daring affairs and notorious infidelity, but she would not listen. Ziegfeld and Burke got married in 1914.

In 1916, Ziegfeld encouraged her entry into movies. In 1922, Billie Burke was voted the public's favorite actress. When Ziegfeld went bankrupt, she bailed him out financially on many occasions. Even after his death, she struggled for years to clear his debts, and was forced out to sell the magnificent "Ziegfeld Follies" to her husband's long time rivals and enemies, the Schuberts. Billie Burke is remembered for her role as the good witch Glinda in "The Wizard of Oz."

*** *** ***

The Ziegfeld Follies Girls.

Florenz Ziegfeld and his Follies Girls!!

More than seven decades have elapsed, yet the name of Florenz Ziegfeld (March 15, 1867-1932) is still remembered as the greatest showman in the history of American theater, musicals and showbiz. What he created was pure magic in motion; his Follies are legendary and his *Show Boat* remained of the most beloved and greatest musical of all time.

In his shows, he glorified the "American Girl." And his stars embodied the essence of sophistication, glamour and showbiz extravaganza. The Ziegfeld Follies Girls were dubbed "the most beautiful girls in the world." They were famous for their beauty, refined silhouette, extravagant outfits, cane and tambourines routines.

The Ziegfeld Girls were famous for their provocative beauty, refined silhouette, extravagant outfits, tambourines routines, and sensual panache.

From L to R: 1-Jean Ackerman, Jean Audree, Myrna Darby and Evelyn Groves in costumes by John Herkrider.

Many of them became famous performers and actresses, to name a few:

Anna Held,
Marilyn Miller,
Barbara Stanwyck,
Billie Dove,
Cyd Charisse,
Dolores Rey,
Gilda Gray,
Gypsy Rose Lee,
Lana Turner,

Paulette Goddard,
Ruth Etting,
Katherine Burke,
Marion Davies,
Gloria Swanson,
Hedy Lamarr,
Lillian Gish,
Norma Shearer.

*** *** ***

Norma Shearer

Jeanne Ackerman, her legs were insured for $500,000.

Fany Brice.
Legend has it that Brice's smile was compared to the Mona Lisa's
mysterious smile.

Introduced in New York City in 1907, The Ziegfeld Follies were produced
every year until Ziegfeld's death in 1932. And continued intermittently until
1957.

NOTES

NOTES

Printed in the United States of America
Published by Times Square Press
New York

1729347R0021

Printed in Great Britain
by Amazon.co.uk, Ltd.,
Marston Gate.